Billy Brownless is a legend. Third on Geelong Football Club's all-time goal-kicking list, he retired in 1997 having played in four losing grand finals. Originally from Jerilderie, he played 198 games over an 11-year career, and considers that his greatest contribution to the game was being decoy for Gary Ablett. For more than a decade Billy has been part of the Nine Network's Logie award winning *The Footy Show*, and is a panellist on *The Sunday Footy Show*. He also co-hosts Morning Glory, a weekday breakfast show on Melbourne radio station SEN1116. Billy lives in Geelong, is married to Nicky and they have four kids – Lucy, Ruby, Oscar and Max.

BILLY'S BOOK  FOR BLOKES

ANTHONY WILLIAM BROWNLESS

ALLEN&UNWIN

First published in 2008

Allen & Unwin
83 Alexander Street
Crows Nest NSW 2065
Australia
Phone: (61 2) 8425 0100
Fax: (61 2) 9906 2218
Email: info@allenandunwin.com
Web: www.allenandunwin.com

National Library of Australia
Cataloguing-in-Publication entry:
Brownless, Anthony William, 1967–.
Billy's book for blokes
ISBN 978 1 74175 570 1
1. Geelong Football Club – Anecdotes. 2. Men – Australia – Social life and customs – Anecdotes. 3. Australian football – Anecdotes. 4. Australia – Sport – Anecdotes. 5. Australia – Anecdotes.
392.36

Cover design by Andrew Cunningham, Studio Pazzo
Text design and typesetting by Pauline Haas, Bluerinse Setting
Printed and bound in Australia by Griffin Press

3 5 7 9 10 8 6 4 2

Here's to all you
Nackers and Cockos out there

Contents

G'day

I'm a bloke. I like a beer and a bet. I love my footy. I love the Darl and my kids. I'm just like every other bloke in this country. I'm more than happy to pay my taxes and I don't reckon I ask for too much in return. If you aren't one of us you probably see it as a pretty simple existence: blokes are just here to eat, drink, breathe and breed. We, of course, know better. There's a lot more to being a bloke than meets the eye.

Traditionally, being a bloke is something you learn on the job. There are no courses you can attend or do over the internet and your own dad isn't that good at passing knowledge on. When you were growing up and doing something for the first time, like using a drill, Dad would only ever speak to you with grunts and shakes of the head. For some reason he always got the most pleasure out of it when you stuffed up. 'That'll learn ya, son.' Dads subscribe to the 'learn through humiliation' theory. If you ever hurt yourself, you wouldn't expect any sympathy from your old man. He'd just say, 'Get up, get back on the bike and get out there again.' In a way it toughened you up. It probably also explains why blokes really don't talk to each other when they've got something on their minds. We tend to bottle things up inside and let them build. As we've grown up, we've been told to deal with things and get on with it.

Us blokes have coped pretty well, all things considered, but I thought to myself, wouldn't it be great to have a book that blokes could turn to as a reference guide. A no-nonsense guide from one bloke to another that doesn't beat around the bush. Let's face it, every now and again we do lose our way. Even if we don't, it's still important to know that you're on track and that everything is as it should be. We've got a lot on our plates. We're husbands, fathers and mates. With that comes a lot of responsibility and commitment. How are we supposed to keep up with it all? That's what this book is about. My thinking was, well if no-one else is going to put out a guide for Australian blokes then why can't I have a crack at it? So I did, and here it is. Everything you need to know. From the rules of backyard cricket to how to give your kids 'the birds and the bees' talk. It's all here.

I'm not in any way suggesting that this is the complete Bible for blokes. (Although, if it does well, they may translate it into 250 different languages. I'm actually fluent in three different languages. Unfortunately, English is not one of them.) It's important to remember that this book is just a guide. It's me, one bloke, sharing my experiences and thoughts with you. You won't agree with everything I say. You may be so offended that you want to punch me in the head. If that's the case, then I'm definitely making you even more of a bloke already.

The other thing to consider is that we're an endangered species, us blokes. That's right, there's this other species of man they've dubbed the 'Sensitive New Age Guy' (SNAG). He's ruining it for all of us with his political correctness, snappy dress sense and use of facial creams. If we're not on the ball and we slip up by not practising long-held bloke beliefs and customs then, heaven forbid, we could die out altogether. It'd be us and the dodo bird and the pack mark. In years to come, people will be ringing the newsrooms claiming that they spotted the once thought to be extinct 'bloke'. That's why it's important to get this book out there and for blokes to read it. It could just ensure that blokes, as we know them, survive.

Blokes have been much maligned for years but the most important people in our lives are blokes: Santa – bloke. The Easter Bunny – bloke. God – bloke. As blokes we have been born with special skills. We can back a trailer, carry four beers at once and hug another bloke without it getting weird at all. As well as this book being a guide, it is also a celebration of blokedom. Stand up and be proud of being a bloke. Pledge your allegiance to other blokes. Shout it out to the world: 'I'm a bloke and some of my best mates are blokes and we're not ashamed of it!' See, you're already feeling better and you haven't even got into the book yet. I just hope my words can make you feel good about yourself. You deserve it. So, to all those blokes out there – this one's for you.

Anthony William Brownless

Dodo (*Raphus Cucullatus*)

The poor old dodo bird is often pictured as an overweight kind of pigeon, and it has become a symbol of extinction, famous for being slow, stupid and fat. Hey, maybe we have a bit in common! Then again, the dodo had wings but couldn't fly, whereas I didn't have wings but some days in the old number 16 jumper I could fly above the pack, no worries. The last dodo died in the late 1600s. We need to make sure blokes don't go the way of the dodo ... hard to stop the slow and overweight part but we can work on not being extinct.

Billy's conundrums

There are a lot of things on this earth that can be explained but many more that can't. For example: Why did I choose football over male modelling? And then there are a lot of rules that we make that just end up confusing us coz they contradict themselves. One thing I remember from school is my English teacher (who, by the way, would faint on the spot if she knew I was writing a book) saying to the class, 'The rule is simple. It's "i" before "e" except after "c".' Then the bell went and we headed off to S<u>cie</u>nce. (How's that? Something I remember from school actually coming in handy later in life!)

I always get stumped by stuff that just doesn't make sense. I ordered a pizza for dinner the other night. I took one look at it and thought to myself, 'If a pizza is round, why does it come in a square box?' and why did I, once again, make the mistake of forgetting to tell them that I wanted a capricciosa *without* the anchovies. Maybe I think too much. (This would be the first time I've been accused of that.) Maybe I'm just a bit of a modern philosopher – opening people's minds to the questions that will unlock the secrets of why we are here. Maybe in the future uni students could be studying the thoughts and theories of one Anthony William 'Billy' Brownless alongside those other famous philosophers from history … whose names I can't think of right now. Hmmm. Probably not.

There are many questions about this world we live in that have me scratching my head – so many of them that I started writing them down. I also began asking friends for things that bug them. If I put them all in one list, it's too much for one man's mind, so they pop up throughout the book when you least expect them. I'm sure you've already asked yourself some of this stuff. Now, thanks to me, you have more questions to clog up your brain.

? Wherever you see this symbol, it's a thing that has me stumped.

Whatever happened to my blond curls? Or, for that matter, to the old hose in the backyard running into the wading pool? These days, I'm bald and you'd have to use old bath water if you wanted to stick your kids out the back in the blow-up pool. Actually, you'd have to have a fence around the pool. Lucky I've still got that winning smile (and that I've stopped wearing romper suits).

Whatever happened to …

There are things that I grew up with that are no longer around or that I hardly see anymore. It saddens me that these things I got so much pleasure out of aren't here for our kids to enjoy – or me, for that matter. Some of them are great Australian pastimes that have just faded away, been replaced by video games or, in some cases, been banned by the government. That won't stop me reminiscing about them and, if necessary, reviving them. That's it! I'm calling up all of my mates and organising a game of British bulldog.

BRITISH BULLDOG

Remember British bulldog? To start with, you needed a grassed area to play on (or asphalt if you were really tough). Everyone would line up at one end and there'd be one guy in the middle. The guy in the middle would call out the name of a person in the line. That person would then have to run to the other side without being caught by the guy in the middle. If he made it, then the rest of the people in the line would run to the other side, trying not to get caught by the guy in the middle. If you were caught by the guy in the middle, then you had to stay there and call out someone else's name. That person then had to run to the other side while avoiding the now two guys in the middle. As people got caught, the number of guys in the middle grew and became harder to get through. Man, what a game. It was a schoolyard classic. A great way to bash into people you didn't like and knock them flying. I once got through an entire lunchtime without getting caught. I was treated like a god at school for the next two weeks.

Unfortunately, British bulldog was banned from most schools by the Fun Police because it was considered too dangerous. They didn't take into account how character building it was. If you made it to the other side, you felt like you could take on the world. There's no doubt that British bulldog is still secretly being played somewhere, especially in its country of origin, England. I've heard that the royal family still play it after Christmas lunch. If the Queen gets a good head of steam up, she's pretty hard to stop. Last year it took five of them to bring her down.

What was the best thing* before *sliced bread?

BRANDY (not what Nanna used to drink)

One of my favourite schoolyard games. One person volunteered or was picked to start with the tennis ball. They would run around and try to hit someone with the ball. Once that happened, they weren't allowed to run with the ball anymore. They had to throw it to each other until they got close enough to hit someone with it. That person would then join them and so on. The only form of defence you had, if you were being targeted, was to use your knuckles to fend off the ball. This was a game of great skill and fitness. You needed everything for this: endurance, pace, evasiveness, hand–eye coordination and patience. This game is rarely seen these days and it's a real shame. It got kids to run around outside and have fun.

The most important thing in this game was to throw the tennis ball really hard at another person. Hard enough that it would leave a mark (hence the name 'Brandy'). If you were feeling in a particularly nasty mood, you would wet the tennis ball. Times have changed though and the Fun Police have been at it again. After abolishing it altogether, they've recently tried to revive the game on a government-sponsored 'Go for your life' fitness website. Here's their new, watered down, soft version. I'm embarrassed.

> **Brandy**
>
> ***Equipment:*** 4+ players (the more the merrier), a tennis ball or a soft foam ball.
>
> ***How to:*** One player is 'it'. That player must chase the other players around the yard or park and attempt to hit them with the tennis ball by using an underarm throw. When a player is hit that player then becomes

brandy and must help get the other players out by hitting them with the tennis ball as well. Remember not to throw the ball too hard at the players!
Who wins: The last person left (non-brandy) wins the game; this person becomes 'it' for the next game.

'A soft foam ball' – can you believe that! 'Using an under-arm throw' – they can't be serious! (OK for Trevor Chappell, I suppose.) 'Remember not to throw the ball too hard at the players' – this must be a joke, right? Half the fun was seeing the grimace on another kid's face after you'd just pelted the tennis ball into that fleshy bit of skin on his thigh. They've turned it into a game for wimps! You either play the game properly or you don't play it at all. What's the world coming to?

Tennis ball

Fun Police approved ball of wool

YABBYING

Yabbying was the best fun. Me and a couple of mates would head down to the local dam and spend the day there. All you needed were some pieces of string, some cut up red meat and Mum's strainer. You'd tie the meat to the string, throw it in the water and wait for the yabbies to bite. Then you'd just scoop them up in the strainer. The easiest fishing you're ever going to do. Unless you lost the strainer, in which case Mum would go nuts.

Yabby
(*Cherax destructor*)

Yabbies are small freshwater crayfish, which make great eating. I'd take a bunch home and Dad would cook them up with his own special recipe, which basically involved him boiling them in a pot of water (that was it). He would also add his own secret ingredient: salt (that was it).

I never hear kids these days say, 'Hey, everyone, let's go yabbying.' I mentioned it once and was virtually laughed out of the lounge room. Our yabbying days were great bonding times. We were also doing something useful by feeding our families. Sure, there were the near tragedies, like the time I put a yabbie down my mate's pants (he still walks with a pronounced lean to one side). But the good moments outweighed the bad by a long way. Sadly, yabbying is a dying art. Which, I suppose, is good for the yabbies.

PLASTIC SOLDIER WITH A PARACHUTE

He was a green plastic soldier, a bit bigger than your hand, with a plastic parachute connected to him by string. A simple toy but easily one of my favourites as a kid. You'd just throw him up in the air and watch him sail down slowly as the air filled his little plastic parachute. If you were feeling especially adventurous, you'd wait till your parents went out and then you'd climb up on the roof and throw him off from there. If you were lucky, you wouldn't end up throwing yourself off there as well. Before too long the plastic parachute would rip and Dad would replace it with a handkerchief. We lost many a good plastic soldier when they failed to return from a mission after being mauled by the dog.

FIRECRACKERS

Again – victims of the Fun Police! If you want firecrackers, you can only get them in Canberra. I suppose they had to come up with a reason for people to want to go there. Now you have to wait for that one bloke from work who makes the trip every year. The day before he leaves he goes around to everyone and asks who wants to put their order in. When he finally returns he's treated like some sort of hero. It's still not as much fun as it was when you were a teenage boy. You could wreak much more havoc back then.

There were these thin cardboard cylinders called 'star shooters' that you'd light and they would shoot out fiery metal balls. When you think about it, probably a bit too dangerous to be put in the hands of a teenager but boy was it fun watching the postman scoot past every day, ducking his head. Penny bangers were beauties. You'd toss one near a group of people and just wait for it to go off. Man, you'd get some good reactions. The problem with penny bangers was that they'd fit nicely through the hole in a letterbox, so a lot of damage was done. I remember my dad on the phone trying to explain to the electricity company that he hadn't paid his bill because the bill had been blown up.

Again, I don't think the authorities thought hard enough about their decision to outlaw firecrackers. As soon as you take firecrackers away from children, you've taken away an opportunity for them to learn how to be responsible.

SLUG GUN, AIR RIFLE OR BB GUN

The slug gun was basically a toy gun that looked like a real gun. You would load it with metal pellets that were great for shooting aluminium cans. We'd have hours of fun doing that. Of course, if you shot a human it would hurt, but it wouldn't break the skin. Just ask our neighbour. We'd lie on the roof and take pot shots at him all day. He'd jump when he was hit but he didn't bleed once. Less of a weapon, more of an annoyance.

?

Why do people squint when they can't see? Wouldn't that just make less space to see out of?

That's what I thought. But no, the powers that be have decided that kids can't play with them anymore. To get a slug gun these days, you need a gun licence. Do you know how hard it is to get a gun licence? You need to be a member of a gun club or have a very good reason. As I discovered, 'taking pot shots at your neighbour' isn't a good enough reason for them. Now lost forever are those skills of composure, sure handedness, a good eye and (in the case of the neighbour) the ability to hit a moving target. I'm not happy.

MARBLES

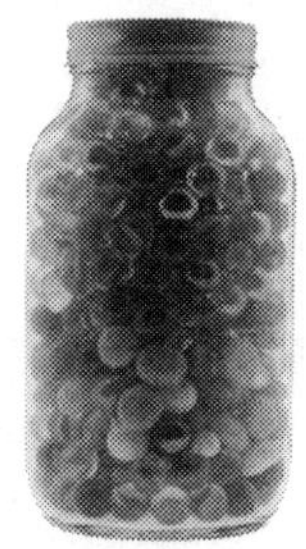

Now, there's a game that was safe and injury free. Except for when you accidentally knelt on a marble and it went right into your kneecap. That was a killer. What I liked about marbles was that there was a reward for winning – you got to keep the other kid's marbles. If you won a lot of them off him then you also got the added reward of watching him cry. The main types of marbles were the cat's eyes, the beach balls and the much sought-after tom bowlers. If you had more than three tom bowlers you were doing well. The main rule to remember was 'No furnudging'. It referred to pushing your hand forward as you released the marble. It was tantamount to cheating. One of the kids at school was a serial 'furnudger' and was banned from playing for a whole year.

?

If marbles aren't made of marble why do we call them marbles?

THE BILLYCART (probably named after me)

All you needed were three pieces of wood, four wheels and some rope and you were well on the way to having your own form of transport. For some reason it was allowed on the road with the other, much bigger, vehicles that were made of metal. When going down a steep hill, the billycart could reach the sorts of speeds Craig Lowndes does but it just fell short in a couple of safety areas such as steering and brakes. There was always an argument about which wheels were the best to use. Old lawnmower wheels or old pram wheels? The general feeling was that pram wheels were faster. We realised we were wasting our breath when the kid up the street flew past us on his freshly made billycart with these small metal caster wheels. They became the must-have item. After we got bored with that, we decided to put shopping trolley wheels on ours. It gave you a real mystery ride. You never knew which way you were going to go.

Unfortunately, the homemade billycart is rarely seen these days. It's a shame because the making of the billycart was a great father–son activity. There was also nothing like learning the road rules while fearing for your life.

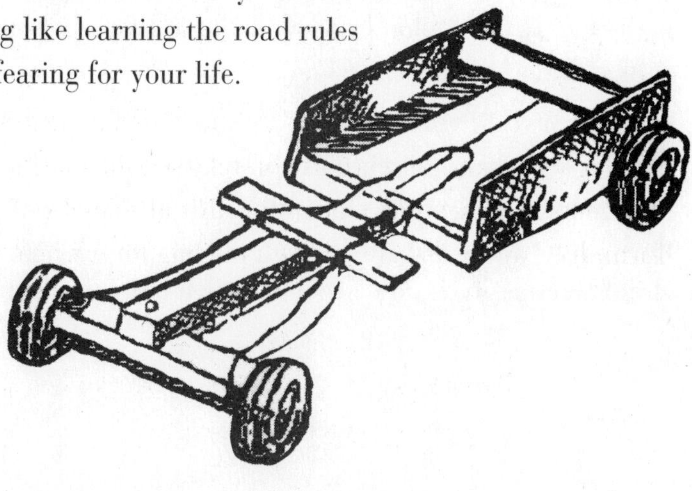

CLIMBING TREES

As a kid there was nothing better than looking up at a big old tree and thinking to yourself, 'I wouldn't mind climbing that.' So, up you'd go. I used to really enjoy it but I wasn't a great climber. I was held back by my big frame and being scared of heights. Other kids, though, would be up the tree and straight to the top in no time. It was a handy skill to have, especially with so many footies getting stuck up the tree. Sometimes you'd get lazy and kick another footy up to knock a stuck footy down. Before too long you had three footies stuck up there, plus a cricket bat, a rake and a broom.

Kids don't seem that interested in climbing trees these days. With all of the other distractions they have, it probably sounds a bit boring. Give me a tree anytime. You can climb it all day at no cost. And a tree will never say 'game over' to you. Unless you fall out and land on your head.

Growing up used to be filled with so much fun and adventure. In those days you couldn't survive without a bike. Everyone had a bike, even the kids who weren't sporty. You spent more time outdoors than you did indoors. Sure, some of the stuff we'd get up to could lead to minor injuries, like grazes, bruises, the odd broken bone and possibly third-degree burns but we were out there, running around and doing things ... and we wonder why childhood obesity is now becoming such a big problem.

Billy's BBQ rules

There's nothing I love more than having some friends around for a barbie, and I know I'm not alone. Over 70 per cent of Australian homes have a BBQ. Like all blokes, I think I'm pretty handy on the old BBQ even though I'm quite crap at it. But we can't help ourselves can we? As men we're drawn to the BBQ by some strange force. It must have something to do with the ritual of the fire and the bonding. I'm not that religious but I reckon the closest I've come to experiencing inner peace and perfect harmony is when I'm holding a beer in one hand and tongs in the other.

Barbies don't just happen. They need planning. A barbie can easily turn into a disaster for any number of reasons and certain systems must be in place for it to be successful. Some of these are food related, some are safety related and some are just good manners related.

BILLY'S RULES FOR PERFECT BBQING

- Before you do anything, make sure the gas bottle has gas in it. Well, when I say before you do anything, I'm assuming you've already put clothes on. There's nothing worse than running out of gas halfway through the barbie. If you do run out of gas and the meat is undercooked, cover it in heaps of tomato sauce to cover the taste. There is no excuse for not having a full gas bottle. You can pop down to the servo where they've got what they call a 'swap and go'. You take your empty gas bottle in and swap it for a full one. As I discovered, after being chased by the guy at the servo, they really need to change the sign to 'swap, PAY and go'.

- Check the weather forecast. It's not much fun BBQing in the rain, and besides, the tongs will get rusty. On the other hand, it may be too hot. If it's a total fire ban, you don't want your barbie being put out by the fire brigade.

- Make sure the BBQ is in a safe position. The following aren't safe: at the bottom of the slide, on top of the rabbit cage, next to an old unexploded World War II bomb.

- Wait 'til the BBQ is really on fire before you put the meat on. It's got to be sizzling hot. A BBQ without sizzle is embarrassing and makes you look very soft.

?

What does the 'K' in 'K-Mart' stand for?

- You must always BBQ with a beer in one hand. Every now and again, pour some of your beer over the meat to marinate it. If you finish your beer, just yell out that you need another one and one will appear in no time.

- Keep raw meats away from cooked meats to avoid any chance of cross-contamination. Don't even put cooked meat back onto the plate it was on when it was raw. The raw juices contain bacteria. And it's not good bacteria like you find in Yakult. Guests will get sick and vomit and then you are going to have to explain to them that they've been spewing up because they've probably had too much to drink.

- The host is the only person who is allowed to touch the tongs unless they delegate some of the cooking to an assistant. Personally, I'm more than happy if another bloke wants to come up and help me out. It doesn't bother me. More often than not, I'll pretend I have to do something and just leave him there.

- If the host has decided that he, and only he, is to do the cooking, then no-one else is allowed to make suggestions as to how the meat should be cooked. They are especially not allowed to utter the following statement: 'You might want to turn them over.'

- There should be a 3-metre exclusion zone around the BBQ that women are not permitted to enter.

- Sausages are only to be cooked one of three ways: burnt, really burnt or cremated.

- Wear appropriate attire for BBQing. You may think you look good in speedos but they're not for around the barbie. The old apron with the boobs on it is way past its use by date. I know some blokes think the plastic boobs are hilarious, which I find quite ironic considering that, in most cases, their own man-boobs are bigger than the ones on the apron. If you want to take the apron boobs joke to the next level, put a T-shirt over the top, wet it and declare yourself the winner of the wet T-shirt competition. [note to cross reference what to wear section]

- BYO drinks is fine but I reckon BYO meat is just rude. It's really hard to keep an eye on it. How can it be fun if people are standing around the BBQ arguing about who brought what? If you're getting people to bring their own food and drink, what are you actually providing? You may as well get them to clean the BBQ and wash the dishes while they're there.

- Kids only get sausages. If they ask for some steak tell them to come back when they're 25. On special occasions they can have onions on their sausages.

- For sausages it's OK to buy the cheapest bread there is. Homebrand is quite acceptable, even if it's a couple of days old.

- As you're cooking, wave your arms about and send the scent of BBQ over the neighbour's fence so that he gets jealous.
- No matter how badly burnt the meat was, everyone must praise the man behind the BBQ for his magnificent cooking efforts.
- Tomato sauce should never, ever run out.

Take pride in your barbie. Never go into one unprepared. A badly organised barbie could have disastrous consequences. Remember, firstly, that we are dealing with a very dangerous substance in gas, and secondly, we need to make sure that our health and hygiene is up to scratch because we are serving people food. The scary thing is that we're doing both these things while consuming copious amounts of alcohol.

A Bill's tour of Australia

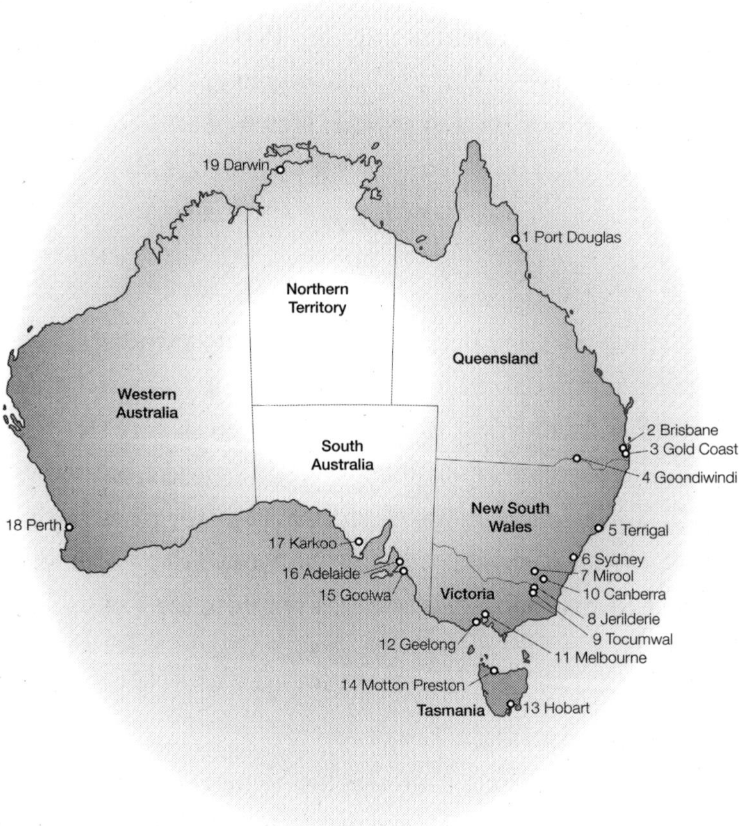

Actually, these are just the spots where I did something really good or the visit was memorable for some reason. Here's a bit of history for you: Thomas Cook (not to be confused with Captain Cook or Brian Cook, CEO of the Cats) was a pioneer of the tourist trade. That's how you get the expression 'a Cook's tour'. So I looked it up in the dictionary and it means 'superficial survey of a place or field of interest'. Perfect! These are places that interest me, and on the following pages I'm giving you a lightweight run-down on them. So it's 'a Bill's Tour'. This could take off – there are too many Cooks, I reckon.

1 PORT DOUGLAS

Golf course. Say no more.

2 BRISBANE

I hold the record for the most goals kicked at the Gabba – 11, to be precise. It was in round 4, 1991, in the days when there was still a dog track around the ground. I hope Buddy Franklin doesn't play too many games at the Gabba – I like holding this record.

3 GOLD COAST

Geelong holds the record for the highest score ever kicked, and we kicked it against the poor old Brisbane Bears at Carrara in 1992. The score was 37.17 (239), I believe. I put Geelong in the record books by kicking a point in the dying seconds. The previous record was 36.22 (238) set by Fitzroy against Melbourne at Waverley Park in 1979. I like to do my bit for history.

4 GOONDIWINDI

Goondawindi, went there with the wheel in 2000 – was that nightmare! It's the home of Gunsynd, the Goondiwindi Grey.

5 TERRIGAL

Went here for the wheel in 2000, they reckon it's magnificent, one of the loveliest spots on the New South Wales Coast. Apparently. I got there in the dark and left at 5 am in the dark. Didn't see a thing.

6 SYDNEY

Blighty had sent me to a fat farm at Pottsville on the New South Wales Coast for five days in an effort to make me get fit. The Cats were playing in Sydney so I got the call to turn up at the SCG. Kicked 9 goals that day. In the reserves.

7 MIROOL

This is where I famously kicked the footy over the silo. I've devoted a whole chapter to this career highlight.

8 JERILDERIE

I'm very fond of the old home town. Kicked my 100th goal there in 1985 as an 18 year old – in fact I kicked quite a few bags of 10 on the Monash Oval. This was named after none other than General Sir John Monash – he went to the local primary school there for a while. He was very famous in his day as an important military man. There's a bit of Australian history for you. When Sir Johnny died, they said he'd be remembered as a scholar, a man of action and an individualist and that he had used his abilities for the benefit of the community. Sounds like me – OK, maybe not

General Sir Bill

the scholar part. But one day maybe I could take over from him as Jeridlerie's best export.

Jerilderie is also famous for the letter that Ned Kelly wrote. Well, he dictated it but there's nothing wrong with that. I probably have a bit more in common with Ned than the General, which is good because Ben Cousins's tattoo has put Ned back in the spotlight.

9 TOCUMWAL

Played in the under-14 Grand Final here, when Jerilderie defeated Cobram. It's the only premiership I've ever won.

10 CANBERRA

Went there on a footy trip when I was playing in Jerilderie – Canberra was like a big city to us. All I remember is everyone driving one way and there were no corner shops or milkbars. Bought home some good videos and firecrackers.

11 MELBOURNE

The MCG is a special place. It's the scene of my career highlights (kicking the goal after the siren and playing in four Grand Finals) and my career lowlights (playing in four losing Grand Finals). Also the scene of the Mighty Cats victory in 2007.

12 GEELONG

Geelong is 75 kilometres down the Princes Highway from Melbourne, via the Westgate Bridge. It's the home of the Mighty Cats, based down at Kardinia Park. Say no more.

13 HOBART

Made a brief comeback in 2000 for my brother's side, DOSA (Dominic Old Scholars v. University). The news that I was pulling the footy boots back on made the Hobart Mercury back page and about 4000 people turned up for the game. I'd blown out as soon as I stopped playing so it wasn't a pretty sight but they raised a bit of money.

14 MOTTON PRESTON

Not the end of the earth, but you certainly can see it from there.

15 GOOLWA

Where the Murray River meets the sea, had a big night with the wheel there. I remember being taken down to some hut ... don't remember much after that.

16 ADELAIDE

No great memories of Footy Park because we never used to win there, but we did do some really silly Blighty warm-ups there!

17 KARKOO

Had an interesting trip here with the wheel in 2000. We flew from Adelaide to Port Lincoln (home of Dean Lukin, the best known weightlifter in Australian history) on Emu Airways (weird name since they can't fly), then drove three hours to the middle of nowhere.

18 PERTH

I have great memories of the WACA ground – we won by a point one night when Blighty was coaching from the boundary line standing on a table. Like a school table. Apart from anything else, I remember thinking, 'Where on earth did he find that table?'

19 DARWIN

One time we were playing in Darwin an Aboriginal lady walked into the three-quarter time huddle saying, 'Where's Gary Ablett? Oh, there's Gary! Hey, Gary!' And Blighty actually stopped talking in the middle of his address and let her have a great old chat to Gary – it was fantastic. I kicked about 8 goals that night. Bloody hot though.

Here's something that defies explanation. How did I become such a champion when I was so far off the mark as a kid?

Sporting things explained

I love my sport. So I should – I'm a bloke who grew up in Australia. It's a given. Never trust a bloke who can't kick a footy or bowl a cricket ball, I say. If I'm ever cutting a deal with someone who is trying to sell me a car or a TV, before I sign anything, I'll chuck 'em a tennis ball and say: 'Let me see you roll the arm over first.' A smooth bowling action and I'm sold! Anything that says 'I bowl like your mum' and I'm outta there. I also never trust a bloke with a moustache. Not sure why. Maybe because I think that he's trying to distract people with that furry little growth above his top lip. One minute you're looking at his mo, the next thing you know, he's ripped you off.

Having grown up playing and watching heaps of sports, I reckon I've got a pretty good handle on most games and their rules. I can spend whole days sitting around and just flicking between the sports channels on Foxtel. If Foxtel can work out a way for the TV to do that automatically as each game gets exciting, then they've got it made. As much sport as I do watch, I still get caught out on a couple of sports that have slipped under my radar. There are also new variations of well known sports that we need to keep up with, as well. That, in a nutshell, is the reason for this chapter. Here are some sporting terms, rules and practices that every bloke should know about. Let's hope my explanations don't leave you even more confused.

TWENTY20 CRICKET

The cricket purists don't like this game but I love it. What is a cricket purist anyway? If they're those stuffy guys with bow ties who sit in the Members at the MCG, then who gives a rat's what they think? Don't get me wrong, I still like watching Test cricket and one-day cricket but Twenty20 just packs all the best things about cricket into the one experience. It's like getting a sausage with sauce, onion and cheese. Basically, everyone loves seeing a batsman smash the ball over the fence. If that's gonna happen more often, it's gotta be a good thing, right? Twenty20 is a much quicker and shorter version of one-day cricket. In fact, if you're standing in the queue for beers for too long, you'll probably miss a few wickets. If you go to the dunny before you buy the beers you may miss an entire innings. This game is fairly new and has only been around since 2005 at international level. I consider myself a bit of a cricket expert but even I wasn't aware of all the rules until I wanted to put them in this book. Here are the rules as far as I can work out.

- Each team bats for a maximum of twenty overs. (Derrrr!)
- Each bowler can bowl a maximum of four overs per innings.

- No more than five fielders can be on the leg side at any time.
- During the first six overs, a maximum of two fielders can be outside the 30 yard circle.
- After the first six overs, a maximum of five fielders can be outside the fielding circle.
- If a bowler bowls a no-ball by overstepping the crease, it costs his side one run and his next delivery is a free hit.
- The batsman can only be dismissed through a run out, for hitting the ball twice, obstructing the field or handling the ball.
- Umpires may award five penalty runs if they believe a team is wasting time.
- If the fielding team doesn't start to bowl their twentieth over within 75 minutes, the batting side is given an extra six runs for every whole over bowled after the 75 minute mark.
- If the match ends with the scores tied and there must be a winner (e.g. a final), then the tie is broken with a bowl-off (like a penalty shoot-out in soccer). Five bowlers from each side bowl one ball each at an unguarded wicket. If the number of wickets is equal after the first five balls per side, the bowling continues and is decided by sudden death.

Instead of a bowl-off, I reckon they should have a 'streak-off'. A supporter from each team must streak to the middle of the ground. The first one to jump over the stumps is the winner. They must also avoid being shirtfronted by Andrew Symonds along the way.

You can't tell me that the cricketing world isn't taking Twenty20 seriously. India won the first ICC World Twenty20 tournament in South Africa in 2007 and the people of India celebrated as if they'd all just been given their very own Ricky Ponting punching bag. Twenty20 is here to stay and in a big way.

THE DUCKWORTH–LEWIS METHOD

While we're on cricket, there's something else that needs explaining. I'm talking about the system they use to decide what score a team batting second needs to make in a rain affected one-dayer – The Duckworth–Lewis Method. No, it's not the brainchild of ex-AFL players Billy Duckworth and Chris Lewis. Two Pommy statisticians called Frank Duckworth and Tony Lewis came up with it. Now, I've read heaps on it and worked out that it can't be explained very easily. These two blokes drew up their own reference table that they need to use, along with a bit of maths. Who said nerds can't have a role in sport? The main thing they base their method on is each team's 'resources' in a match. The resources in a cricket match are the number of overs a team has to face and the number of wickets they have in hand. With 50 overs and ten wickets in hand a team has 100 per cent of its resources available. Anything less than that will be a lower percentage of resources. They can work the percentage out by checking on their reference table and this then helps them to work out the target score. I still don't know exactly how it all works and probably never will but Steve Waugh reckons that it's the best and fairest method there is. If it's good enough for one of this country's greatest captains and all-time legends, then it's good enough for me. I've decided to put The Duckworth–Lewis reference table in the book coz it can also be used to calculate how many beers you need to drink per innings.

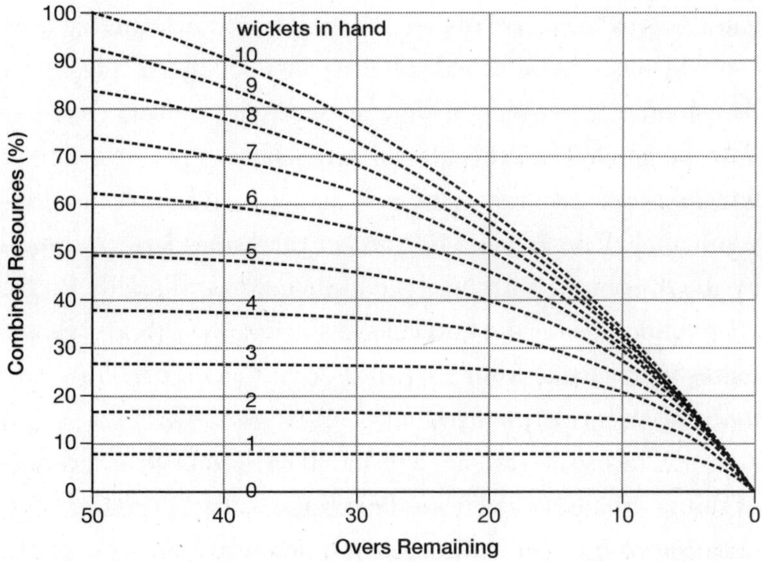

TENNIS

Yes, we all know how to play tennis. I'm not questioning that. Australia has a rich history in the sport. Our own Rod Laver is regarded by many as the greatest player of all time. They named the main court at the Australian Open after him. I think it was out of him and Damir Dokic. Even though we've grown up with the game, many of us still don't understand why the scoring system is what it is. Where did 'love', '15', '30' and '40' come from? The short answer is that no-one is exactly sure but there's many a theory floating around like a mongrel punt.

From what I've read, some people think that the origins of the 15, 30 and 40 scores go as far back as French medieval times (that's going back 500 years). They may have used a clock face on the court, with a quarter move of the hand to show a score of 15, 30 and 45. When the hand moved to 60, the game was over. Other people say that the scoring could've been copied from a game called sphairistrike, which was played by British officers in India during the nineteenth century. Not sure how the game went but the scoring was based on the different guns of the British naval ships. When firing a salute, the ships would fire their 15-pound guns on the main deck, followed by the 30-pound guns on the middle deck, and finally by the 40-pound guns on the lower deck. Personally, I reckon that if tennis scores came from old sailors then there'd probably be a lot more swearing involved.

The use of 'love' for zero could have come from a couple of things. Some say it's from the French word for 'egg' (*l'oeuf*) because an egg looks like the number zero (and my head). Another theory is that 'love' could've come from *'l'heure'* or 'the hour' in French. The word 'deuce' comes from the French word *'deux'*, meaning 'two'. That's enough with the French. Up until now the only French I'd used was 'croissant' (you know – the pastry. Not even sure if I spelt it right). Remember how your mum used to say, 'Don't use words if you don't know what they mean.' Well, now when you're playing tennis and yelling out the scores – you know what they mean.

AMERICAN FOOTBALL (GRIDIRON)

Many of us have become more interested in this game since some of our own AFL players have made it over there. Benny Graham is playing for the New York Jets and Sav Rocca is at the Philadelphia Eagles. They're both punters because of their ability to roost the ball a long way. Mmmm, I wonder what those Yankee talent scouts would've thought of a young kid from Jerilderie who could kick a football over a wheat silo?

I've got to admit, American football looks pretty impressive with those guys running around wearing helmets and the kind of big shoulder pads that my mum wore in the '80s, but how exactly does this game work? And why do the players have to invent a new dance every time they score a touchdown? Well, let me try and tell you, in simple Billy language, what this game is all about.

The game is played on a 100-yard field with an end zone of 10 yards at either end. That's 120 yards in total. It is just over 53 yards wide (remember a yard is just a bit bigger than a metre). This is a lot smaller than your average AFL ground (Telstra Dome is 160 metres long and 129 metres wide)

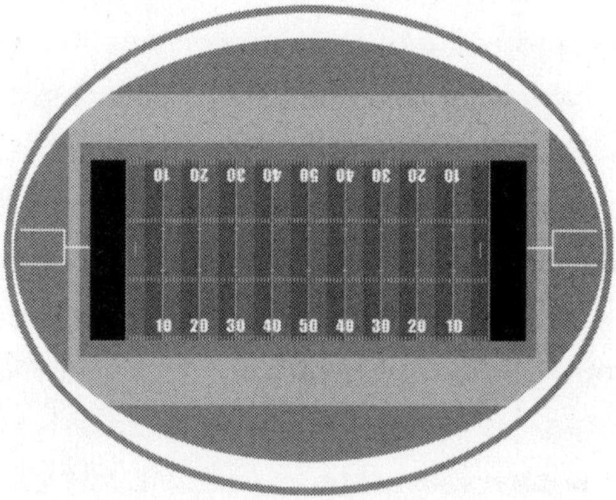

but pretty close to the same length as the SCG. (Just kidding Sydney! But let's face it, I reckon you could just about have a shot at the other goals if you were kicking out after a point.) The object of the game is for your team to move the ball down the field and into the opposition's end zone – to score a touchdown (worth 6 points). Your team gets four chances to move the ball 10 yards. Once you move it at least 10 yards then you get another four chances to move it another 10 yards and so on. If you don't make the 10 yards, then the opposition gets the ball (after someone, like Ben Graham, punts it back to them). You can move the ball by running with it or throwing it to someone who catches it. The quarterback is the player who controls your team and he hands the ball off to someone to run with it or throws it to a receiver who catches it. Unlike rugby, where you have to touch the ball on the ground to score a try, in American football the ball only has to break an imaginary plane, which goes from the goal line straight up into the air. Once you have scored a touchdown you then get to kick the ball through the goal posts (uprights) to score an extra point. Instead of a touchdown you can also score by kicking a field goal, which is worth three points. Even though there are eleven players for each team on the field at one time, each club has many more players because they really have three different teams. One for offence, one for defence and one for special plays (catching the kick-off or punt and running the ball back down the field). Some players are in more than one of these teams. Some players, like Ben Graham and Sav Rocca, come onto the field, kick the ball and then go straight off. Like most American sports, they have rules and systems in place for convenience's sake.

The National Football League is divided into two conferences. At the end of the season, the winners of both conferences play-off in the Super Bowl. It was half-time at a Super Bowl when Janet Jackson controversially exposed her nipple. (Then again, I had both my nipples out by quarter-time in Geelong's grand final win.) There's other stuff you need to know but I'll let you pick that up when you watch the game.

Do they need all of that padding? Is it tougher than Aussie Rules? It probably is now. It wasn't in the days when Stan Magro shirtfronted Jezza. But that's since been outlawed. What about the fancy touchdown dance celebrations? Well, they've been outlawed over there now. I think one player did the Nutbush and the authorities had no choice but to step in.

I've watched Ben playing on the telly. Like the other punters, he does the torpedo type spiral punt but it's a real buzz when he throws in the odd drop punt (or 'end over end' as the Americans call it). I'm just hanging out for when he introduces the American game to the infamous 'banana' kick.

?

Why is it that it's good to be under par in golf
but it's bad to be under par in any thing else?

TEXAS HOLD 'EM POKER

Before you jump down my throat and say 'Poker shouldn't be classed as a sport!', too late! I've already decided that it is. It's on ESPN, so it must be. Texas hold 'em poker has taken off in a massive way in the last five years. There are different forms of poker but this is the one that you see on TV and that everyone is playing now. New Aussie hero, Joe Hachem, won 10 million bucks playing Texas hold 'em. It's a great story. He was keen to head over to the States to try his luck and his wife said, 'Sure thing. Off you go.' She must have read a different Wife Handbook from everyone else. What a woman! No wonder he did so well, he was under no pressure. Some blokes struggle to get their wife's blessing to go to a poker night at their mate's place, let alone on the other side of the world. In the end, it paid off. I'm sure Joe would've bought his wife a nice bunch of flowers out of that 10 million he won, or at least thrown her a couple of fifties and said, 'Go buy yourself something nice.'

Texas hold 'em, or just Hold 'em, as it is also known, can be played with anywhere from two to as many as 22 players. Each player initially gets two cards which only they see. Three community cards (shared by all players) are then flopped, face-up in the middle of the table. During two more rounds of play, two more community cards are flopped. Players bet in between and win by making the best five card poker hand using their own two cards and three of the community cards. Here is a more detailed guide as to how a game would run.

1 One player starts as the dealer and it rotates clockwise after each hand. The two players to the left of the dealer are the 'small blind' and the 'big blind'. These players place bets

before the cards are dealt. The bet amounts are agreed upon by the group. The *small-blind* bet is almost always half the big-blind bet. So, for example, if the table limits are $2/$4 and the big blind is $2, the small-blind bet is $1. The *big-blind* bet amount is at the low end of the table's betting limit. For example, if the table betting limits are $2/$4, the big-blind bet is $2. If the limits are $100/$200, the big blind is $100. They're called blind bets coz no-one has seen their cards yet. After a few beers there'll be plenty more blind bets of another kind.

2 Each player, including the dealer, is now dealt two face-down cards ('hole' or 'pocket' cards). Don't show anyone your cards or try and look at another person's cards. If you ask them what they've got and they're stupid enough to tell you, then that's OK.

3 The player to the left of the big blind is the first player to act on the starting hand. This player has these options: **Bet or raise.** Blind bets are already on the table, so this player cannot simply *'check'* (pass the play on to the next player without betting). He must match or raise the bet on the table. If he is raising and the table stakes are $2/$4, the player must match the big-blind bet of $2 and add another $2 for the raise. Most games allow a maximum of three raises per betting round before raising is *capped* or stopped. Or, **fold or muck his hand.** If the player does not like his cards and doesn't want to play the hand, he can fold his cards, drop out and go straight to the fridge.

4 The play moves around the table until all players, except the small- and big-blind players, have had a chance to act on their first two cards. When play comes to the small-blind player, he has these options: **Complete his small-blind bet to a full bet and play the hand.** For example, on a $2/$4 table, the small blind is $1. In order for the small-blind player to play this hand, he has to add another $1 to his original bet to complete the bet to a full bet of $2. Or, **raise the pot by completing his small-blind bet to a full bet and adding another full bet for the raise.** For example, on a $2/$4 table, the small-blind player is in the hand for $1. If he wants to raise, he would bet an additional $1 to complete his original bet to $2 and add another $2 as the raise, making a total bet of $4. Or, **fold his hand and give up his small-blind bet. If you're not sure what to do, you can always go the fourth option, which would be to pretend you just got a message on your mobile, so that you can stall for time.**

5 After the small-blind player has acted, play comes to the big-blind player. This player has already made a complete bet in the blind, so he has these options: **Check his hand because he is already in the play, having made a full bet on the blind**. Or, **raise the pot by making an additional full bet**. Or, **call a raise if another player acting before him has raised the pot**. In thinking about these options don't give away your feelings about your hand by sweating or shaking so much that you're spilling your beer.

?

Why is it called 'after dark' when it is really 'after light'?

6 After every player around the table has had a chance to act on their starting hand, the next round of play – called the 'flop' – begins. The dealer burns a card (takes it off the top of the deck and puts it aside) and then flops three community cards onto the table (face up). These three community cards now become part of everyone's hands. Don't ever pick these cards up and hold them next to yours just to see how they all look together. Not cool.

7 Betting action starts with the first player to the left of the dealer and moves clockwise around the table. Players can choose to check their hands and pass the betting option to the next player. After a player does make a bet, checking is no longer permitted and all subsequent players must match the bet, make a raise, or fold their hands. This is where the game becomes tense, so start humming a really annoying tune, just to mess with your mates' heads.

8 After all players still contesting the pot have had a chance to act on the flop, the dealer then burns another card and turns a fourth card face-up on the table. This card is known as the 'turn' or 'fourth street'. Betting starts again with the first player to the left of the dealer who's still in the hand, and moves around the table. On this round (and the final round), the minimum bet doubles in size, so in a \$2/\$4 game, the minimum bet on fourth street is \$4. After a bet has been made, players must match the bet, make a raise or fold their hands. If you opt out here, make sure you slam your cards down hard, messing up everyone else's piles of chips.

9 After all remaining players have acted on fourth street, the dealer burns another card and deals the last card face up, known as the 'river' card or 'fifth street'. Players now see all the cards that will be dealt in this hand, and they must make the best five card hand out of the seven cards dealt (the five community cards on the table and their two pocket cards). The final round of betting begins the same way as before, with the first remaining player to the left of the dealer checking the hand or making a bet. All players still vying for the pot must also bet, raise or fold their hands. If you're still bluffing, this is the point you start pooping your pants.

10 After the betting round is complete and more than one player is still vying for the pot, all active players have a 'showdown' and turn their cards over. The player with the highest poker hand made by using any combination of the five community cards and two pocket cards wins the pot. To rub it in, the winner should make a rectangle out of his arms, lean over the table and rake all the money towards himself, while making the noise of a front-end loader.

As an added bonus and to refresh your memories, opposite is a list of poker hands in order of best to worst.

Hopefully, I've provided you with everything you need. Except for the nibblies and drinks and I'm not chipping in for those. The most important thing to come out of this is that you don't have to feel like a bit of a dick when you sit at a Texas hold 'em poker table anymore – because now, you know your 'flops' from your 'turns'.

Winning hands

Royal flush	This is the best hand in poker, consisting of 5 cards in sequence from Ace to 10, all in the same suit. I've never had one or seen one.	A♠ K♠ Q♠ J♠ 10♠
Straight flush	This is a combination of a straight and a flush. How did a toilet term make it into cards?	8♦ 7♦ 6♦ 5♦ 4♦
Four of a kind or Quads	Having 4 of any one rank.	J♣ J♦ J♥ J♠
Full house	This hand consists of 3 of a kind plus a pair.	8♥ 8♠ 8♦ 4♣ 4♥
Flush	Having 5 cards of any one suit.	Q♣ 10♣ 7♣ 4♣ 3♣
Straight	Having 3 cards in a rank sequence.	J♥ 10♣ 9♥ 8♠ 7♠
Three of a kind	Having 3 of any one rank.	5♦ 5♠ 5♣ A♠ J♦
Two pair	Having 2 different pairs (also how many undies I own).	K♠ K♦ 9♠ 9♣ 2♦
One pair	A single pair.	Q♠ Q♥ J♠ 6♠ 3♦
High card	High card hand is the lowest non-pair hand.	A♦ 10♠ 9♦ 4♠ 3♥

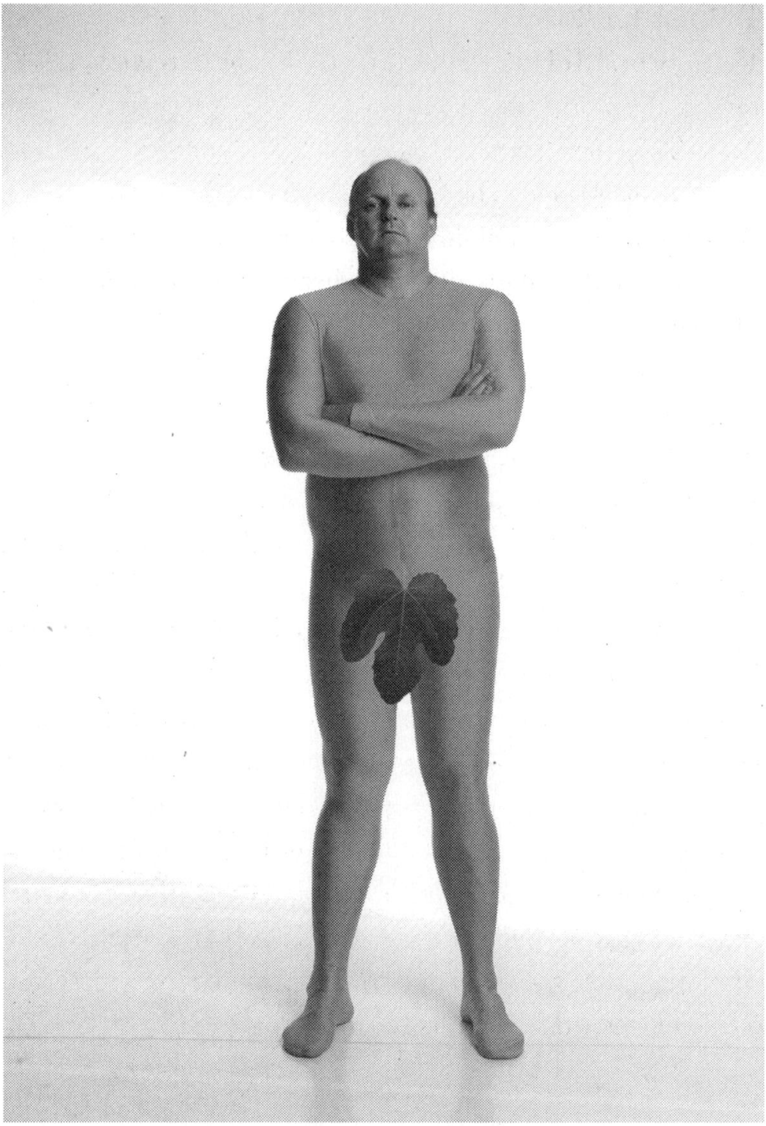

I had to do a bit of bike riding for a wheel segment on Channel Nine. If you're riding a bike, you have to wear lycra, right? WRONG. It's OK for the professionals on the Tour but that's all. I had to endure jokes about 'no meat' and 'no potatoes' for days afterwards.

TOUR DE FRANCE

We've all heard of the Tour de France. It's the most famous bike race in the world. We see it on the news, especially when an Aussie is up there with the leaders. In 2007, our very own Cadel Evans came second. The highest finish ever for an Australian. We know that there are different coloured jerseys and different stages and that, recently, dogs have been introduced as obstacles, but there's a lot more that we don't know.

The race goes for 22 days and has twenty stages in it. It is run over 3000 km, throughout France. The riders are in teams of nine and each team is known by the name of its sponsor. There are usually around twenty teams. Traditionally, entry to the race is by invitation only but if you want to try and gatecrash it on your BMX – good luck.

We're all familiar with the yellow jersey. The bloke leading the race wears it. There's also the green jersey, for the rider leading the sprint points (points are earned for place getting in each stage). Less well known is the polka dot jersey (I'm not kidding – it's white with red dots) which is worn by the leading hill and mountain climber. (You'd be letting someone else pip you at the post to avoid having to wear that one.) And the leading rider under the age of 21 wears the white jersey. After the 2007 race, I'm sure they're coming up with a new jersey for the rider who hits the most dogs.

Why is it called a TV 'set' when you only get one?

RUNNING OF THE BULLS

Sure, not a recognised sport, but close enough. You have to run and pretty bloody fast at that. So, just go with me on this one. There are running of the bulls festivals in a lot of Spanish towns but the most famous of them all is held in Pamplona. A lot of Aussies have it down on their 'To do' list. I think visiting Gallipoli is No. 1 and Pamplona No. 2.

The bulls are run through the streets to the bullfighting ring to mark the start of the nine day festival. The run is about 800 metres long and the participants wear the traditional white shirt and pants with a red waistband and scarf. Wooden barricades are put up to direct the bulls along the route and to block off side streets. There is a double row of barricades at five places along the way so that runners can escape. Stories from Aussie first-time runners tell of how they tried to climb over the barriers only to be pushed back in by locals.

Personally, I don't like bullfighting, it's cruel and should be banned. That's why, when I watch the Pamplona run, I always barrack for the bulls. They're always good value. Without fail, each year they'll give you something to cheer about. Heaps of people and some bulls get injured every year. Since 1924, fifteen people have been killed in the run, the most recent being an American tourist in 1995 (even bulls can't stand American tourists). If you're going to tease and torment the bulls, you deserve everything you cop, I reckon.

As a protest to the run, animal welfare groups have started the 'running of the nudes'. It takes place in Pamplona two days before the running of the bulls and it's just people in the nude running. It has helped raise awareness of the cruelty of bullfighting and it's a lot less dangerous, although some dangly body parts could take someone's eye out. I'm putting the running of the nudes on my 'To do' list. It's a good cause. Let's hope I don't get my dates wrong and end up butt naked being chased by some bulls with really big horns.

The Brownless theory of evolution

1. Footballer *Infantis*
No muscle development, not much hair, but a keen look, and signs of confidence in front of the camera.

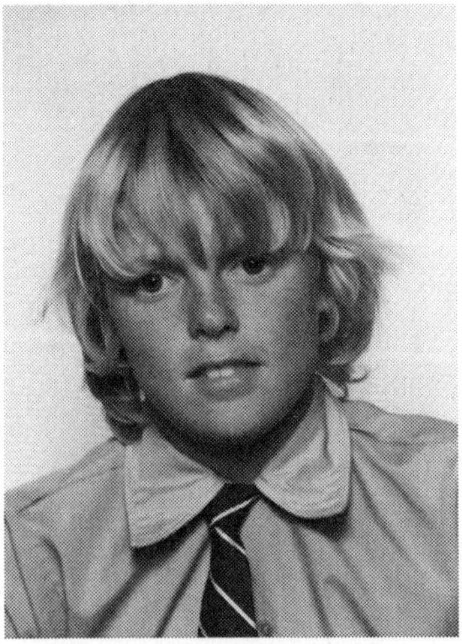

2. Footballer *Pubis*
Environmental influence is evident in the shirt and tie. You can tell I'd be more comfortable in footy shorts but I've adapted to social conditions imposed (i.e. school).

3. Footballer *Adonis*

Social influence is a big thing in theories of evolution. I have now crossed over into the *footballer* category. I've already mastered the sexy pose in front of camera in order to attract the female species.

4. Footballer *Adulecens*

There are two sides to the development of *footballers*: external (physical) and internal (spiritual). This shows very good development on the physical side. Nice muscle development in the shoulder area. Still plenty of hair.

5. Footballer *Athleticus*

Now, footballers are not generally big on the internal development side of things, but this is evidence of my belief in my own kind of higher power. Spiritually guided by Blighty, I believed I could fly.

6. Footballer *Decoyus*

As physical skills fade, the *footballer* must adapt to his limitations. I found the perfect role – decoy. This extended my football career by a good ten years (and I only played for eleven).

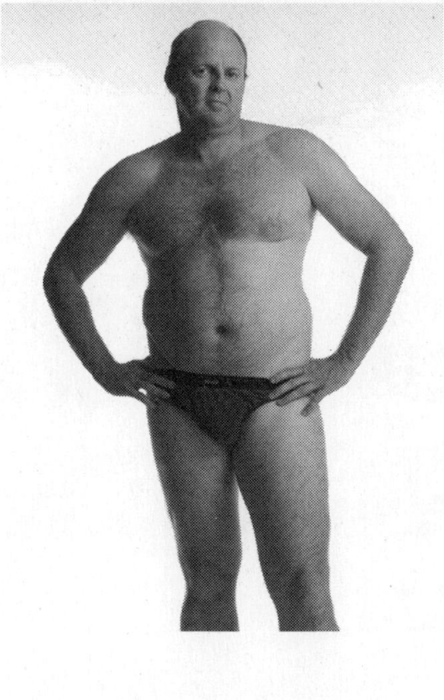

7. Footballer *Finitis*

This is the full evolutionary circle: back to no muscle development and not many feathers left!

Blighty, holding his huge brain in place while he works out the next training drill.

The Wisdom of Blighty

All the great leaders, thinkers, inventors and artists throughout history were geniuses in their own right but they also had one other thing in common – they were all nut cases. It comes with the territory. Malcolm Blight was a great leader. The best coach I've ever had. Yep, he was a nut too. More-knowledgeable people liked to use the word 'eccentric'. A brilliant coach, with a record to match, Blighty was known for being a bit 'out there'. His coaching methods were, in a word, different. Some of the things he got us to do as players were inspiring and yet often embarrassing. His ideas fit somewhere between groundbreaking and just plain ridiculous. Even sitting here and writing a few of them down, I still can't believe that they happened or that I was there at the time and agreed to do some of them. But there was method to his madness. He took a rough bunch of wannabe footballers from down Geelong way to three grand final appearances between '89 and '94, and then coached Adelaide to back to back premierships in '97 and '98. We can all learn a lot from someone like Blighty. With a bit of luck, the stories I tell in this book about the great man will see some of his wisdom rub off on you.

The year is 1991. We are about to play Richmond at home, one winter's day in June. It's just like any other normal pre-match preparation. The players start drifting into the rooms a couple of hours before the match. You can hear the buzz of the Geelong faithful as they're arriving and the atmosphere is beginning to build in the special way it always does at Kardinia Park. It's a tough task for any team to travel down the Princes Highway to Geelong and try and take the points. Richmond are going to have their work cut out today.

It's about an hour and 15 minutes before the bounce and we're thinking about getting changed into our footy gear, when Blighty walks in and tells us all to go to our bags and pull out our towels. The next thing you know, we're walking out of Kardinia Park. You can imagine how it looks to our supporters, who can see us all leaving, still dressed in our civvies and carrying towels, as they're just coming in to the ground. They're all looking at us and saying, 'What's going on with you blokes?' We're looking at them, going, 'We don't know, we're just following the cockroach.'

Outside, Blighty has organised for a bus to be waiting for us. So we all troop onto the bus and it drives off. We hit the streets of Geelong which, by now, are becoming clogged with footy traffic. The players are sitting in their seats thinking, 'We've got a game to play in an hour and we're on a bloody sightseeing tour.' After driving around for a while, the bus slows down as it approaches this big double storey place. Someone recognises it as the house of a well-known supporter. The bus pulls up at the house and Blighty orders us to get off. We all file off the bus with our towels in tow, wondering what the hell we're doing here.

We walk up the long driveway, past the well-kept gardens, and are directed around to the back of the house. When we get around the back we find a fairly decent sized swimming pool. Obviously Blighty has thought to himself, 'Oh well, something different. They're not expecting this. I'll make 'em swim up and down the pool on a freezing cold day in June. That'll get their blood flowing.' I don't know about getting the blood flowing coz just the mere thought of jumping into that icy water was starting to get the shrinkage going.

So there we all are, standing on the paving around the pool, waiting for our next instruction. Now, whether Blighty changes his mind or just wants to keep us guessing, I'm not sure, but he then ushers us towards some big sliding glass doors near the pool. We walk through the doors and into this big room. It's like a big family/rumpus room, with a wooden floor and a bar in the corner. Still carrying our towels, we are told to sit in a circle on the floor. Blighty then makes us put our towels on our heads. We look at each other for a few seconds, shrug our shoulders and put our towels on our heads. 'The towels on your heads,' he says, 'represent the feathered headdresses of the American Indian Chiefs.' Blighty's vision is starting to become a lot clearer now. We're the 'Indians' going out to battle against the 'cowboys' (Richmond) and this is our big 'pow-wow' before the battle.

Before you have a chance to jump out a window and yell 'Geronimo', Chief Blighty moves himself into the middle of the circle and produces an imaginary peace pipe. His mime work is

?

Where do all the daylight saving hours go?

something that has to be seen to be believed – a gift that would make any street performer jealous. After he has a good puff on the imaginary peace pipe, he gives it to our captain, Mark Bairstow. He also has a puff before passing it around the circle for us all to have a go. Some players have big imaginary peace pipes. Some have small ones. Some blokes look like they're sipping a slurpee. I have a puff and blow out some imaginary smoke footies. Eventually the peace pipe makes its way back to Chief Blighty, who then orders his Indians to get back on the bus. The preparation is complete. We are ready for war. Look out General Custer! We head back to our rooms, get stripped and run out onto the ground with fire in our bellies.

Richmond beat us that day and like in an old western, the Indians had lost again. But not all was lost. I, for one, had learnt a lesson – never smoke before a game.

Billy on tools

I've got a shed and I've got tools in it. I've got a shadow board to put all the tools on and it looks great. That's where many of us stop. We don't use the tools as much as we should but we still go out and buy more and stick them up on the shadow board. We go into the shed every day just to look at the shadow board and admire it. That, in itself, is more than enough for some of us. That's what we grew up dreaming about. Anyone who so much as moves a tool or doesn't put it back in its right place, is in serious trouble. The rest of the shed, mind you, is an absolute mess.

Not all of our tools are brand spanking new. There are those ones that were handed down to us by our dads. Whenever they buy a new tool, instead of throwing the old one out, they give it to us. My dad gave me his old drill. Our fathers always stressed the importance of safety when it came to tools yet they're more than happy to give us an old rusty drill with a damaged cord that could potentially kill us at any time. Here's a word of advice for fathers thinking of dumping their old tools on their sons: if a tool is no good for you anymore then it's probably no good for anybody else.

We've all got our favourite tools. Some we can't live without and others we just enjoy using. They're like a sports car that you take out for a drive on the weekend. Some tools we get very attached to and treat as members of the family. There are also those tools that keep playing up to the point where they drive us mad. They're only hanging around until hard rubbish day. I've come up with a list of what I consider to be the top ten tools. Remember, this is just my list. Your list might differ. If it does then you need to take a good hard look at yourself.

BILLY'S TOP TEN TOOLS

10. Measuring tape

This gets a hell of a workout at my place. I'll get an idea and bang, I'm measuring stuff up and writing down the measurements. We all do a heap of measuring but how often do we actually follow it up? In my case, almost never. But geez, I've had some good ideas. Sometimes you even manage to drag someone else into it: 'Can you hold the end of the measuring tape for me?' The measuring tape also comes in very handy for measuring the kids' heights as they grow up. Every year, on their birthday, we put a mark on the back of the kitchen door. We've even got heights on there for some of their imaginary friends. The best thing about the measuring tape is how, with the flick of a switch, it recoils back all by itself. True, you think

you're going to lose a finger each time it comes flying back, but they're the sorts of risks you're prepared to take as a home handyman. If you want to be a real thrillseeker put the vacuum cleaner next to the measuring tape and recoil the vacuum cleaner cord and the measuring tape at the same time.

9. Level

I don't know how they got that bubble in there either but the bubble don't lie! I love using the level. I put it on all sorts of stuff. If I'm sitting down and looking over at a door frame and wondering if it's level, I'll just grab the level and find out for myself. 'Yep, that's level. Anything else you want me to check while I'm here, Darl?' I like the way the bubble keeps you in suspense by going back and forth before settling in its spot. One day I'm going to break the glass and set the bubble free.

8. Hedge trimmer

I've got an electric one and it trims real good. My problem is that once I start trimming, I don't know when to stop. I always need to cut a bit more off this side to even it up and then a bit more off the other side. Before you know it, I've completely butchered the tree. What started as a minor trim has turned into 'short back and sides'. Let's face it, put the hedge trimmer in my hands and I'm out of control. Even my little dog quakes in his boots when he sees me coming. He thinks he's going to be next. Now that I've recognised the problem, I should be able to deal with it.

7. Saw

Cutting wood with a saw has a special rhythmic feel to it. You can really get into a good groove of going back and forth with your arm, as the saw cuts deeper into the wood with every stroke. Sometimes I don't need any wood cut but I'll just cut some anyway coz it's good for the soul. There are different saws for different jobs. The hacksaw is used for cutting metal. Nowhere near as much fun as cutting wood. It's fingernails on the blackboard stuff. There's also a tree saw that you use for cutting branches. Never, ever use the wrong saw for a job. It could have dire consequences. According to statistics, the chance of divorce increases after a wife uses a hacksaw to cut a tree branch.

6. Socket and spanner set

These are cool. They come in their own little carry case and without fail, after three days you've already lost a couple of pieces from the set. I'm not up with what all the different sizes are but the ability to loosen and tighten bolts is what separates us from the rest of the animal kingdom (I think). No matter how many years I've been doing it, I still have to stop and think to myself, 'Right, to tighten I go clockwise … or is that anticlockwise? Hang on, isn't that to loosen …?'

If you haven't got a socket and spanner set then you can get by with a shifter. What a top invention. Instead of lots of different sized spanners, why not have one spanner that can adjust to different sizes? Brilliant! How come we don't

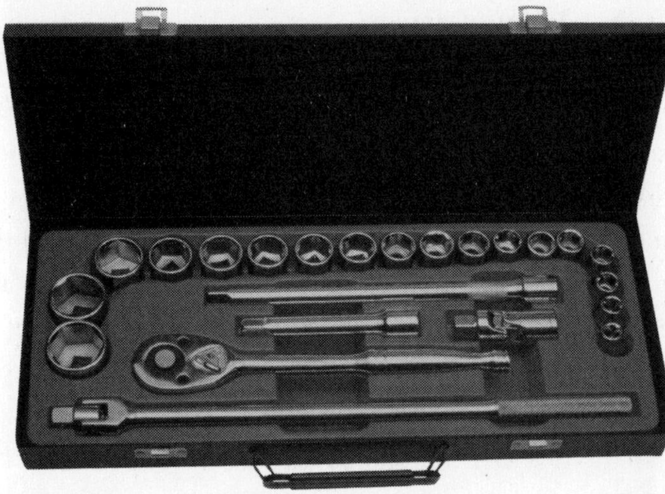

know this guy's name? I want to meet Mr Shifter and shake his hand. We should be studying him at school. Forget the guy who invented the telescope. How many bikes has that fixed? None!

5. Drill

Every bloke has to have a drill. It's a must. There's a great sense of raw power that comes with holding one in your bare hands. There's always something around the house that needs a hole drilled into it. Walls inside your house are a big worry because blokes often don't get the first hole right. They miss the stud. The next thing you know there are seven holes in the wall. You then have to hope that the picture frame is big enough to cover them all. It begs the question, what's the more damaging pest in a house – a white ant or a bloke with a drill?

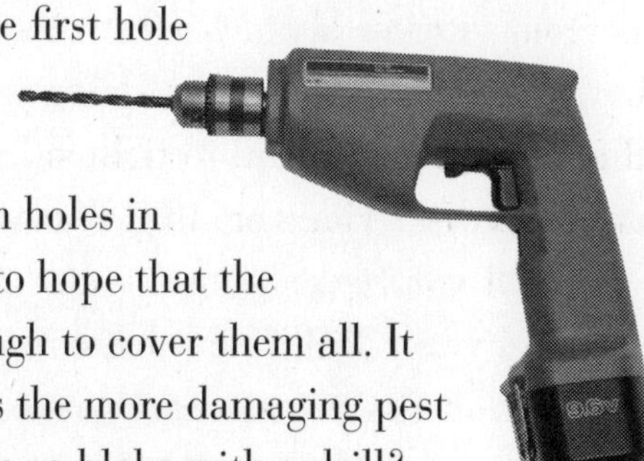

4. Screwdriver

There are two main types. The flat head and the Phillips head. The Phillips head was named after Henry F Phillips, an American businessman (he must've had some weird looking head). He tried to patent the idea but it was so heavily copied that it was impossible to patent. Poor bastard. I mean, every household must have a Phillips head screwdriver. It's more important than a kettle, a toaster, an oven, a fridge or a car because they're all held together by Phillips head screws. I've got a Phillips head screwdriver placed in every room of the house, just in case of an emergency. The flat head screwdriver does have one thing over the Phillips head. It can open a paint tin. Just remember not to stir the paint with it.

3. Leaf blower

This is easily one of my favourite things in my shed. It's a controversial inclusion. It's not really a tool in the old-fashioned sense but boy is it fun to use. Crank it up and it just blows stuff. Anything from leaves to the kids on the swing. Some people say it makes us lazy; I say it makes us more efficient. We now have more time to do other handyman jobs. I recently discovered that my leaf blower has reverse. That's right, it sucks stuff as well. The potential is endless. I could sit inside, in my lounge chair and never have to get up to get anything ever again.

?

How can they be called 'safety pins' when you're always pricking your fingers on them?

2. Crowbar

A simple tool but very effective. Whatever you choose to do with it, the crowbar is designed to cause maximum damage in the process of doing it. It's great for opening stuff. You just might have trouble closing it again. It'll open anything. You name it. Jammed doors or windows, old wooden chests, car boots, stubborn milk cartons. You can also dig holes with it. It goes into the ground so easily. Not sure what you're going to do with all of the holes in your backyard, but worry about that later. It's also a great weapon for self-defence. Whack someone over the head with a crowbar and they ain't getting up. When religious nuts come knocking, answer the door brandishing a crowbar – they won't hang around.

1. Hammer

The humble hammer is my No. 1 tool. It's the most basic of tools and one of the world's oldest but it's the most essential. There's no better way to get in touch with your manhood than by banging a nail in with a hammer. And if you stuff it up, the claw on the back can fix your mistake by pulling the bent nail out. It's like a tool version of white-out. I've built on my hammer collection. I started with a dad hand-me-down hammer and now I have three. I want more. I'm becoming an obsessed collector, just like Angelina is with kids.

The hammer is a survivor. It was challenged by the nail gun and survived. It had its name tarnished by MC Hammer and survived. It's still with us for good reason. There is no other tool that fits so comfortably in a man's hand. It's the most natural feeling tool we have. Long live the hammer.

The importance of different tools varies from bloke to bloke, depending on what they like doing. Some blokes like the noise, muscle and energy that come with a power tool. Some blokes get a buzz from pulling a cord to get their tool started. Some blokes like the simplicity of using an old-fashioned hand held tool. Man has a special relationship with his tools. It's something that only he understands. This dates back a long, long way. Tools have been around since caveman days. We know this because archaeologists dug up a prehistoric Bunnings catalogue.

Kicking the goal after the siren

Picture this. It was 9 September 1994. Geelong v Footscray, qualifying final, MCG, big crowd in attendance under lights.

I'd had a pretty dirty night playing on Danny Southern and he'd told me before the bounce that if I touched the ball too many times he was going to punch me in the head so I took his word for it and didn't go near it. Anyway, very late in the game we were a point down, and I said to myself, 'Gee, you've gotta do something here, Billy boy.' So I lead out with my superior pace and took a magnificent pack mark against three or four Footscray players. And sure enough, the siren went. So there I was, 45–50 metres out. We needed a goal to win, a point to draw, and I had the footy. I was on the wrong side for my right foot and the ball was pretty heavy coz there had been a bit of rain around that night. It was going to take my best kick.

People always ask me what I was thinking about but I wasn't thinking about anything. I remember lining up for goal, and Tony Liberatore saying things about my mother that

?

Can a pig pull a hamstring?

Never in doubt!

I didn't think she could possibly do, but I put all that out of my mind and went back, just doing my normal routine. I was confident I could do it.

Then BANG! The best feeling in the world was watching that ball sail through those goals. We'd won! And it went about 30 metres past the goals so I reckon I kicked it about 80 metres in total!

And then – and I don't know why – I just ran and ran and ran. It was first time I'd ever run 50 metres on the MCG without getting caught. Then John Barnes got hold of me and kissed me on the lips (and if you know where Barnsey's lips have been you'd be worried about that too). And of course all the boys were grabbing me and even Blighty was trying to get into the action, coming over the top of the pack.

We all had a few beers on the way home. But I couldn't sleep – I couldn't wait to read all about in the paper the next day. So I got up early and went down to the local paper shop and banged on the door to see if the *Sunday Herald Sun* was in but I was way too early. In the end I had to go home and wait hours till it was delivered.

It's one of my great memories of playing football and it still sends shivers up my spine whenever I watch it.

Trust me. I'm an ex-footballer. Everything I know I learnt from Blighty.

Community service

Don't get the wrong idea about the title of this chapter. It's not referring to a community service order imposed on me by the courts. I'm not one to run afoul of the law. When it all boils down, I'm a pretty sensible bloke really. Sure, I've had too much to drink on the odd occasion, may have woken up in a complete stranger's lounge room and possibly run naked through Germany but other than that, I've kept out of trouble. The community service this chapter's about is the work I did in my role in the PR department down at Geelong. The club somehow thought that I would be a good ambassador. I enjoyed the job. It was a great opportunity for me to put something back into the club that I love.

As part of my duties one day, I had to go and visit an old people's home. When I arrive I'm met by this bloke in a suit who works there. He tells me to follow him down the hallway. I haven't seen an old person yet but I know I'm in an old people's home because they have a certain smell to them.

?

Why do supermarkets put in so many checkouts when they only have 3 or 4 open at one time?

You know, that stale smell of clothes that have been around for nearly a century mixed in with the smell of old skin falling off. Yeah, that smell.

We walk through some double doors and into the main rec room. It's a big room with bright lights, a wooden dance floor in the middle and colourful curtains. There's a big picture of the Queen on the wall (didn't realise she was staying there) and there are old people everywhere. There's a vibrant atmosphere in the room. They're having a great time and involving themselves in all sorts of activities. They're chatting, drinking tea and playing cards and they're all decked out in Geelong jumpers, scarves and beanies. Some have pompoms and streamers. It's a sea of blue and white.

I get up and have a chat to them, talk a bit about the mighty Cats and answer a few questions, mainly about Gary Ablett. What's Gary Ablett like? Do you know him well? What does he like to do? Why didn't he come today? What sort of car does he drive? Is he part robot? While I'm going through all of this, I notice one old woman, who's not in Geelong gear, sitting by herself in the corner of the room. She's not paying any attention to me at all, in fact, she couldn't be less interested. When I'm done, I'm going to have to go over and have a word with her, I think. I just want to see if I can connect with her and at least make her smile.

So, I wander over and sit down next to her. That smell I mentioned earlier has really kicked up a gear where she is. I politely say, 'Excuse me.' In a craggy, grumpy voice she goes, 'What?' I say, 'Do you barrack for the Cats?' She goes, 'No!' I say, 'Do you like football?' She goes, 'No!' I say, 'Do you know who I am?' She looks me up and down and says, 'No, but if you ask the nurse, she'll be able to tell you who you are and take you back to your room.'

Yep, this old lady had my measure. Time to go. When I went back to the club, I got the players to sign a Geelong jumper and organised for it to be sent to her. A month later we got a message back from her saying thanks and that it's now her favourite cleaning rag.

How to dress

Let's be honest, what to wear and when isn't high on our list of priorities. Some blokes don't care to the point where they're happy to leave it up to the Mrs to decide. I'm sorry but that's a cop out. I reckon we have to take a bit of control back. In saying that, we do really need a refresher course because when it comes to clothes, we still have a lot of bad habits. The only reason people keep buying us undies and socks for our birthday, Fathers' Day and Christmas is because they're sick of seeing us walking around in our old ones which are full of holes.

Men usually get dressed in the following way: Open the drawer, grab whatever's on top and put it on. If the drawer's empty, then look for the pile of your dirty clothes on the floor or on the side table. Pick an item from there and give it the smell test. Spray with deodorant if unsure. If it is wrinkled, don't iron it, just stretch the garment with your hands. Any creased business shirts can be hung on the clothesline and gently sprayed with the hose. Last of all, never worry about whether your clothes match. And that's pretty much how we do it. We've been getting away with it (just) for years but it's not ideal. The older you get the more functions and events you have to go to. Each of these requires a bit of thought to be put into what you wear. Fortunately, I've done most of the work for you. I've gone through the various occasions you're likely to attend and suggested what outfits you should wear. Here's my take on it all.

BLACK TIE

Some weddings or other functions may be black tie. If you haven't got a formal black tie suit then you'll have to borrow one off a mate or hire one. In which case, you'll have to be extra careful not to make a mess of yourself. You don't want to have to pay for it to be replaced. The AFL has enforced the black tie rule for the Brownlow Medal (anything to avoid a repeat of Graham Teasdale's velour suit in the '70s). But don't feel restricted by the black tie dress code. It doesn't necessarily mean the old winged collar and bow tie job. The AFL players have already set some new trends with their cool Brownlow black tie suits. The long thin black tie seems to be all the rage at the moment. See, Billy's up with what looks hip. The only problem is finding something my size.

MCC MEMBERS

Neat casual with minimum requirements. Why is this in here? Well, most of us at some stage get to go into the Members at the G as a guest of a member. Unfortunately, many of us are refused entry because we're not aware of the dress code. Males fifteen years and over must wear a collared shirt. If you're without one then you'll have to buy one from one of the club merchandising stands. If your team isn't playing that day then you could end up paying money for a Collingwood shirt and then having to actually wear it. Jeans are acceptable but they cannot have any tears or holes in them. You can wear runners but no thongs, scuffs, dilapidated footwear, gumboots, moccasins, slippers or ugg boots. Whatever you're wearing, it's very important that, while you're in the Members, under no circumstances are you to ever take part in a Mexican wave. If caught in the act, you'll be taken down to the bowels of the grandstand where you'll be tortured and/or shot.

AT THE RACES

Classy/trashy. It all depends on where you are for the day. If you're in the Members or in a marquee then you'll need to be in the latest suit. It's high fashion stakes here. Even last year's suit might be out of date. Trust me – and it pains me to say this – you may have to buy a new suit every year. If you're in the public area then it's open slather. It's all about coming up with a good idea and running with it. If you're with a group of mates then it's acceptable to dress in the same outfit. The following are pretty popular: superheroes, jockeys, horses, nuns or just generally in drag.

AT THE FOOTY

Comfort. You must be comfortable. You'll be sitting there for hours, plus the train trip. A team scarf is your best bet. It shows where your allegiance lies without going overboard. Wearing your team jumper shows commitment but at what age should you stop wearing it? Personally, I reckon there needs to be a cut-off point. I'm making an executive decision right here and now that the cut-off point should be 30 years of age. Any older and it's starting to look a bit tragic. It's also a lot more difficult to get into bars later that night and it severely reduces your chances of picking up.

There's a whole colour section later in the book featuring me – all dressed up, right through to almost undressed – that you can use as a guideline for various occasions. The idea with this picture section is that it's stuck randomly in the book so you have to read other bits on the way to finding it. Other bits that are GOOD FOR YOU, like the prostate check-up chapter. It's like going to IKEA where they make you walk for miles through stuff you think you don't want on the way to finding what you went there to get.

Anyway, once you've taken my advice on board you should have new-found confidence in your fashion sense. Just don't be seen to be spending too much time on it. It's not a good look for a bloke. Act naturally. It's as if you've never even read this chapter. In fact, rip the colour section out now and destroy it.

Cooking with beer

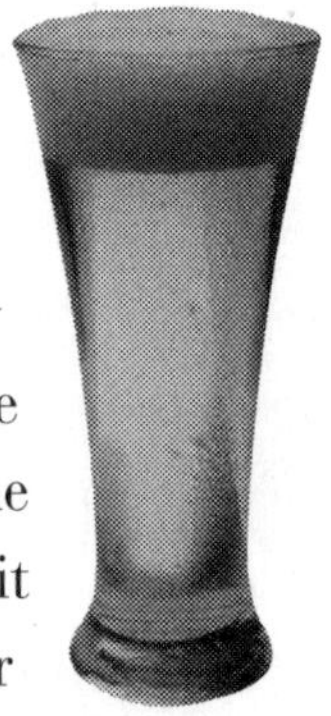

We all look forward to a beer (or a few) at the end of the week. We've earned it. Beer has those two special qualities about it. It tastes good and makes you feel good. Like most of us, I don't know exactly how or why it does it. I haven't got a degree in beerology. I just know it does it. That being the case, why not incorporate beer into our diets a bit more? A lot of people mightn't be aware that beer can be used in cooking. And if anyone's going to be the ambassador for that idea, who better to do it than me? I'm even prepared to make big statements about it. By the year 2010, I want to see beer in every kitchen cupboard in Australia, sitting proudly on the shelf next to the olive oil, soy sauce, vinegar, basil leaves, coriander and leuenberger. (Not sure but I think that last one may be a footballer.)

I'll be honest, I'm not the greatest cook going around. Don't get me wrong, I'll have a crack [the Darl says, 'Bullshit! Never happened and never will!'] but when it comes to success rate in the kitchen, I'm on a par with Glenn McGrath's batting

Why are the small chocolate bars called 'fun size'? Wouldn't it be more fun to eat a big one?

average. What better way to motivate me and the thousands of hopeless bloke chefs around the country than by bringing beer into the equation? We can make it the next big thing in cooking. Who knows, one of you out there could become Australia's leading beer chef.

This chapter is not about me being blokey and having beer in everything just for the sake of it. Beer is actually really good in cooking. It adds flavour, it helps tenderise meats without breaking them down as much as the acidic wines and vinegars do, it's cheaper than wine, and the dark beers, like your stouts, can stop those dangerous bacteria that cause food poisoning. Don't worry, I'm onto all this stuff, trust me.

Now, I've made sure that you have no excuses for not giving beer a go in the kitchen. I've gathered a few beer recipes for you to try. Don't go nuts on it. Slowly introduce it into the family diet. If you're having beer on your cornflakes, then you've gone too far. And remember, when it comes to cooking, if more beer is going down your throat than into the food, then chances are it could be a shemozzle. Good luck.

BEER BREAD

By adding a few ingredients to a can of beer, you can cook yourself up some delicious beer bread. Best eaten straight from the oven. Any leftover beer bread should not be fed to ducks.

Ingredients

4 cups plain flour
2 tablespoons baking powder
2 teaspoons salt
¼ cup sugar
350 ml beer (NOT light beer)
2 eggs, slightly beaten

Method

Mix flour, baking powder and salt with sugar. Add beer and egg both at once and stir. You may have to knead last of flour in with hands. Place in a greased 24 cm x 12 cm loaf tin and bake at 190°C until done – about 1 hour and 10 minutes. Remove from tin and let cool. Great for toast as well.

BEER MARINATED BAKED CHICKEN WINGS

Give those chicken wings a bit of flavour by having them soak in beer overnight. Try soaking in beer yourself overnight, it'll do wonders.

Serves 4–8, depending on when you serve them

Ingredients

¼ cup olive oil
½ cup beer
¼ cup light soy sauce
⅛ cup lemon juice
½ teaspoon salt
¼ teaspoon pepper
⅛ teaspoon ground ginger
1 clove garlic, minced
16–20 chicken wings

Method

Combine all ingredients except chicken and blend well.

Rinse chicken under very cold water. Drain on paper towels. Place in a large bowl or plastic bag and pour marinade over wings. Turn all pieces to coat thoroughly. Cover tightly and refrigerate for 24 hours.

Place chicken skin-side up in a roasting pan. Discard excess marinade. Bake at 180°C until golden brown, about 1 hour. Delish!

BEEF IN BEER AND ONIONS

Beef is slowly braised with onions and dark beer until it is tender. The onions and the beer combine to create a rich and flavoursome natural gravy.

Serves 6

Ingredients

1.2 kg chuck or round beef cut into 6–8 slices
salt and freshly ground black pepper
2 tablespoons butter
2 tablespoons olive oil, and a bit more
5–6 medium onions, peeled and thinly sliced into rings
1–1 ½ tablespoons flour
2 cups dark beer
2–3 sprigs fresh thyme (or 1 teaspoon dried)
1 bay leaf, crumbled

Method

Cover both sides of beef slices with salt and pepper. Add butter and olive oil to a frying pan and brown meat for a couple of minutes on both sides. Remove meat, cover it and set aside.

Add a bit more oil and sliced onions to a pot. On a low heat, sweat onions until soft and lightly browned, stirring often. Add flour to onions. Cook, stirring constantly, until flour is lightly browned.

Add beer to onion and flour, stirring until thickened Add thyme and bay leaf. Put beef into pot and cover. Cook over low heat for about 2 ½ hours, until beef is really tender. Check often to be sure beef is covered in liquid, adding more beer or water if necessary. Serve with rice and salad. Yummo!

BEER BOILED PRAWNS

Prawns and beer have always complemented each other, so why not chuck 'em both into the same pot? This recipe is pretty straightforward – even I couldn't stuff it up.

Serves 6

Ingredients

2 cups dark beer
2 small onions, peeled and sliced
1 clove garlic
1 bay leaf
3 whole peppercorns
2 celery stalks, cut into pieces
2 teaspoons salt
½ lemon, quartered
1 kg raw prawns, cleaned

Method

Pour beer into a large pot and add onion, garlic, bay leaf, peppercorns, celery and salt. Bring to boil, then simmer for 10 minutes. Add lemon and prawns and simmer for another 12 minutes. Remove from heat, drain and let cool. Peel off shells from boiled prawns, leaving tails intact. Arrange around a platter with tails up and your favourite dipping sauce in the middle. Place lemon wedges around sauce dish. Pig out!

BEER BATTERED TOFU – FOR THE VEGOS

It hurts me to put a vego recipe in here but I know there are a few of you out there (most of who were unwillingly converted by their partner). So, what better dish to do for vegos than tofu?

Serves 4, or more, you need a lot to fill you up

Ingredients

1 can cheap beer
1 ½ cups plain flour
1 cup cornmeal
1 tablespoon paprika
1 tablespoon garlic pepper seasoning
1 tablespoon parsley
¼ teaspoon salt
½ teaspoon garlic powder
1 package (450 g) drained firm tofu or extra-firm tofu
¾ cup canola oil
tartare sauce or sweet chilli sauce to taste

Method

Mix beer and flour in a bowl. Adjust consistency until it looks like a thin pancake batter.

In a second bowl, mix cornmeal, paprika, garlic pepper seasoning, parsley, salt and garlic powder.

Cut tofu into approximately 1.5 cm-thick slices. You should end up with about 10–12. Place slices on a piece of paper towel then place a couple of paper towels on top and pat to dry a bit. Carefully dip slices of tofu in beer batter, shaking off excess. Place in cornmeal mixture and tap each side to get coating to stick.

Place in hot oil in frying pan until golden, about 3 minutes each side. Remove from pan and place on paper towels to drain. Serve with tartare sauce or sweet chilli sauce. Question your manhood and then enjoy.

WHOLE CHICKENS COOKED ON A BEER CAN

This is from *Huey's Best Ever Barbecue Recipes* (now there's a good bloke, Iain Hewitson).

Serves 4

Ingredients

2 handfuls of woodchips
1 large chicken
1 can beer
spice mix (try McCormick's spicy Italian)
olive oil spray
2 handfuls baby rocket
olive oil
balsamic

Method

Soak woodchips overnight. Set kettle BBQ to indirect grilling with large drip tray in the centre. Open beer and drink half. Insert can in the chicken's cavity and spread legs so that it will be steady on the grill.

Sprinkle generously with the spice mix and place chicken upright over drip tray. Put a handful of drained chips on each bed of coals, cover and cook for about 45 minutes, spraying every now and then with oil.

When ready (check by piercing thigh with table fork – if it's cooked, the juices should run clear) remove can carefully, joint and serve with a pile of oil and vinegar dressed leaves.

A very useful story

Me and Gary Ablett had to do a coaching clinic for the local kids down Geelong way. I knew there would be heaps of kids there, wanting to get their photo taken with us and get the great man's autograph – and Gazza's too – and he wasn't the most reliable bloke round the club, so I thought I'd go round early and pick him up.

We jump in the car, and on the way to the ground we go past a TAB. Gazza says, 'Hey, pull up here, I wouldn't mind a bet. I've got a good tip.' Footballers think they get all the inside info because they know trainers and jockeys and get all the mail. So he boxes up 5 horses, gets the trifecta and wins $1200. It's fair to say Gazza was tight with his money so he was pretty happy with his win. He gets the girl behind the jump to count out the twelve $100 notes, goes over to a little table, counts them all out to himself just to make sure they're all still there, and goes back to girl and asks her for a rubber band to keep the notes together. He rolls them up in the rubber band, puts them in his pocket, and away we go, off to Kardinia Park to teach some kids a thing or two about footy.

?

Can a bald man ever have a hairline fracture?

There are about 300 kids there, all decked out in their Geelong gear. We have to split them into two groups: 298 kids go with Gazza – they all want to be with him – and the three of us in my group have a great old time, with plenty of handballs and kicks. There's a huge line behind Gazza. The kids in his group hardly get a touch.

I notice one little boy who looks like he's come from a struggling background. He has holes in his old Geelong jumper, he's wearing green footy shorts and different coloured footy socks and his parents obviously couldn't afford footy boots. He has runners on and the sole of one of them has nearly come off – you can hear him flapping around.

At the end of the clinic, we call them all together to say a few words of encouragement, and I go first. 'Well done today, boys and girls, you were all fantastic.' I tell the kids to eat their veggies, do their homework, don't drink, don't smoke and so on. That's what you do when you're an AFL player.

Then Gazza gets up. 'Well done today guys, great work. I want to make special mention of one boy here.' And of course he points to the little boy down the back of the group, in his old jumper, green shorts, odd socks, and the runners. Gazza says, 'Come up here, mate.' So this kid flip-flop-flip-flop-flaps all the way to the front.

'Well done, kid, I thought you were great today and I'd like to help you out.' And out of his pocket comes the $1200. Crikey! I cannot believe it! Gazza's going to give this kid $100 for a new pair of footy boots! That's fantastic!

With that, he pulls the rubber band off the money, throws the kid the rubber band and says, 'Here, wrap that around it, that should fix it.'

That's our Gazza.

* **Disclaimer:** Apologies to Tony Shaw who I reckon told this story about Darren Millane – I'm pretty sure I pinched it off him. And then Aker pinched it off me a few months back. Feel free to make it your own – it's a good, clean multi-purpose story.

Get your prostate checked

There's no point beating around the bush in putting a title to this chapter. Get your prostate checked now! In fact, do it right now. Put this book down and call this number: 1800 220 099. Go on. Do it!

You're still reading, aren't you? I'm serious. Put the bloody book down. I'm waiting ... still waiting ... Look, I know the thought of another man putting his finger up ya pooper isn't the sort of thing that would normally inspire you to pump your fists in the air, jump in the car, bounce into the doctor's surgery, drop your dacks and yell, 'Righto, who wants to inspect me clacker?' but the consequences of not getting it checked could be a lot worse.

Nearly 3000 men die each year from prostate cancer in Australia, which is at the same level as breast cancer in women. Over 18 000 new cases of prostate cancer are diagnosed every year but it can be cured if detected and treated early. Who would have thought that such a little-known gland would cause us blokes so much trouble? What exactly is the prostate gland, I hear you ask? I'm about to tell you. Well, try to tell you. I'm no medical expert. When I left school I wouldn't have minded having a crack at being a doctor but they weren't taking on apprentices.

I have read up on this a bit, and I will try and explain what the prostate is in simple terms, so that we both understand.

A bloke's plumbing

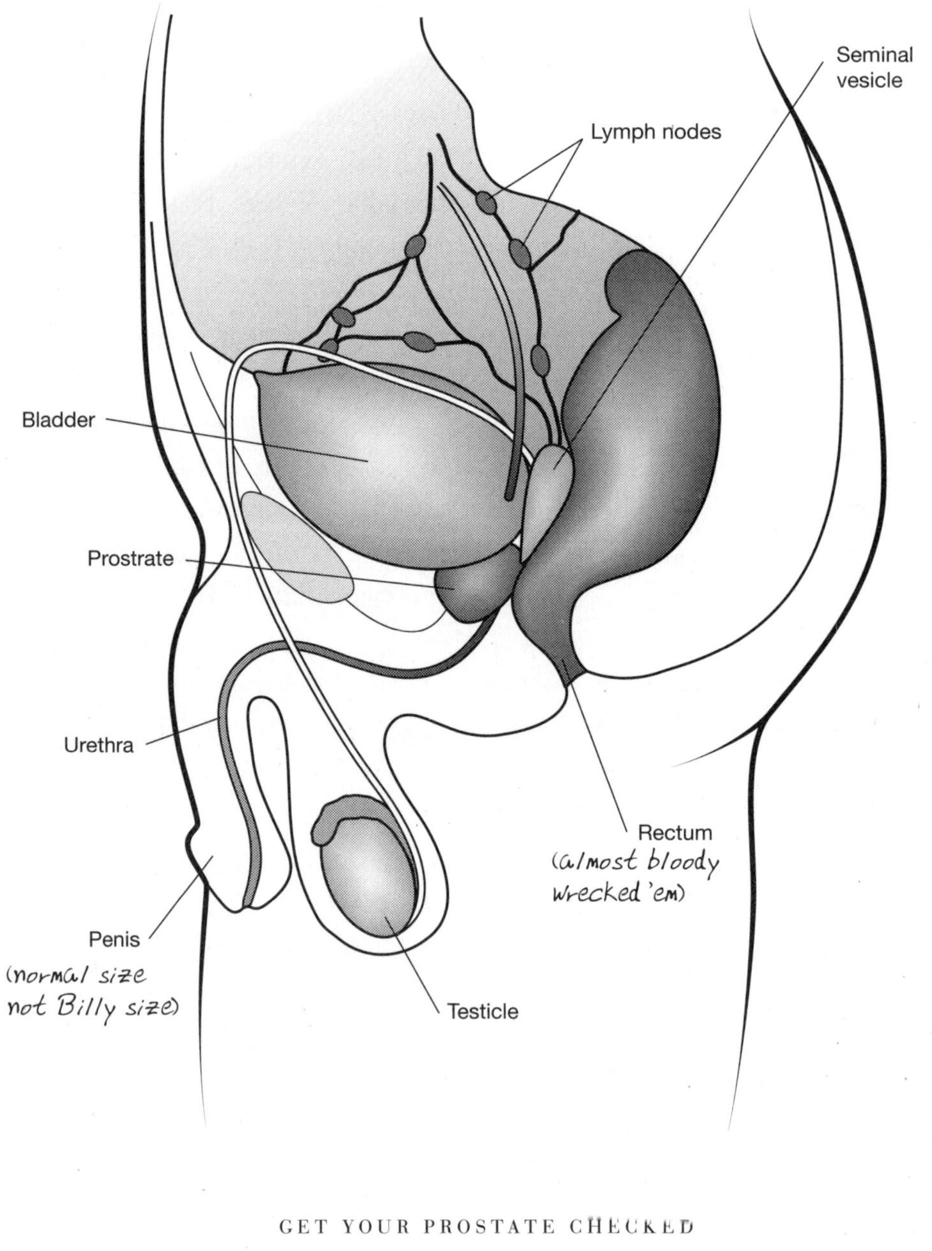

So, here goes. The prostate is a donut-shaped gland that sits underneath the bladder and has an opening into the urethra (the tube that takes your urine from your bladder to your penis. See diagram). The main role of the prostate is to add a milky fluid which protects and enriches the semen. As you can see, it does play a very important role, but one which can go unnoticed. A bit like a half-back flanker who keeps pumping the ball forward, only to sit back and watch the full-forward get all the credit. But if that half-back flanker becomes enlarged then that is going to have a negative impact on the rest of the team … mmmm, nice work Billy! So, don't be a 'half-back flanker' and go and get it checked, will ya!

If your prostate does become enlarged, there are some symptoms you can look out for:

- waking frequently at night to urinate
- sudden or urgent need to urinate. (Ignore these first two if you've had a big night out on the frothies.)
- slow flow of urine
- blood in the urine or semen
- trouble starting to urinate
- discomfort when urinating

Why is it called your 'bottom' when it's in the middle of your body?

- painful ejaculation
- decrease in sex drive
- difficulty maintaining an erection. (Erection problems can be caused by other things, like nerves. I recommend having a couple of frothies to help you relax. Not too many, though. You don't want the old 'Foster's flop'.)

If you have any of these symptoms then don't panic. There are heaps of non-cancerous problems that can affect the prostate. Your best bet is to see your doctor and have yourself checked out, especially if you're over 40 and have a history of prostate problems in the family. Anyone over 50 should get themselves checked out anyway.

Take it from someone who knows, 'the finger up the bum' isn't as bad as it sounds. Yes, I must admit, when I first thought about having it done, it did freak me out. As far as I was concerned, my bum hole traffic was 'one way only'. It's an exit. Nothing was allowed to travel in the opposite direction. 'Wrong way, go back!' But when it comes to your health, you need to loosen the road laws a bit, so to speak. If you think it's going to be awkward for you, imagine how the poor doctor feels. They've studied their brains out for six years at uni so that they can now stick their finger up someone's arse. If you

How can a nasal spray fix something as far away down your body as an erection? If you're having nose problems can you then spray something down your pants?

still have concerns, talk to your doctor about your worries. Ask them any questions you might have, so that you are more comfortable with the procedure. As I said to my doctor before he started my examination, 'Hugh, I hope you've cut your nails.' Some men prefer a female doctor. Their fingers are generally a bit smaller. Every millimetre counts. Whatever it takes to get you down to your doctor – do it. Your health should always come first.

I also stumbled upon another interesting fact while reading stuff on this topic. Prostate problems are less common in Chinese, Indian and Japanese men. Doctors believe it has something to do with the way they go to the toilet. Most Asian toilets are squatting toilets. Just a hole in the ground that you squat over. We, on the other hand, use a sitting toilet. Sitting actually puts more strain on our insides as we try to force our waste out. Squatting is how we are naturally designed to go to the toilet, as it relaxes those parts of the body we use. Have a think about that the next time you lock yourself in the dunny for half an hour. I won't be taking the newspaper in there to read anymore either.

I've been lucky enough to have been involved in the EJ Whitten Legends Game, which raises money for prostate cancer research. You can't buy the sort of publicity this yearly event has brought to the cause. Since it began in 1996, the EJ Whitten Legends Game has raised over $730 000. In 2007 the match was televised live for the first time and won the

?

Why do they call it 'taking a dump'? Shouldn't it be 'leaving a dump'?

ratings for its timeslot on the night. I'm surprised Channel Ten didn't try to buy it and turn it into a reality series. I ran around for a few of the games but soon realised that I was kidding myself. My injury-riddled body means that I now struggle even to kick the cat. My exit, though, paved the way for the new generation of broad-chested champion – Bryan Strauchan. The kid can play. His physique and the way he moves out on the ground remind me of a young Brian Taylor. I certainly miss rubbing shoulders with some of the game's greats, especially at the bar after the match. We would have a couple, then have a couple more, before kicking on and partying so hard you'd think we'd just played a game for the West Coast Eagles.

The EJ Whitten Legends Game pays tribute to the spirit of Ted and it's appropriate that he is remembered and celebrated in such a way. Regarded as one of the greatest footballers ever to play the game, EJ was a fighter from a working class background, who always showed the type of toughness needed to tackle such a disease. He was a great man and his passing stunned us all.

I'd written this bit before I learnt of my old mate Sam Newman's battle with the disease. And because I knew more about prostates than I ever had before, it was all the more scary to find out that someone as fit as Sam could get it. Just goes to show that we should all be on our guard. Sam allowed the TV cameras in to film his procedure, which is a great way to keep prostate cancer in everyone's minds. His private life is constantly in the public eye anyway, so Sam probably thought, what the heck. Good on him, I say.

There are certain things in life that we can and cannot control. Football players on an end of season trip – you cannot control. Taking care of your health is something you can control. So, make an appointment with your doctor. What are you waiting for?

Some important football history. Ted Whitten was a legend of the game in the truest sense of the word. You don't get called 'Mr Football' for nothing. On 17 June, two months before his death, the G was charged with emotion of a different sort as EJ made an almighty effort to do a final lap of honour before the State of Origin game against South Australia, accompanied by his son, Ted Jnr, and his grandchildren. There wasn't a dry eye in the house. Prostate cancer even got the better of this toughest of tough men so get your prostate checked now!

Going to the tip

As a kid nothing excited me more than Dad waking us up in the morning with these words: 'Boys, today we're going to the tip.' You could tell what we were doing just by looking at Dad because he was wearing his tip clothes. They were an old set of clothes that he only ever pulled out when he was going to the tip. A bit like Batman only ever putting on the tights and the cape when he was fighting crime. Dad's outfit wasn't as flash but he did once wear his undies on the outside by mistake.

There's something magical about going to the tip. It's an adventure. That's how we saw it. Dad saw it as an opportunity to use his kids as slave labour for the day. We'd get up early and spend hours doing backbreaking heavy lifting and loading the trailer and we didn't even care coz the payoff at the end was going to be worth it. If you were lucky, Dad would whet your appetite by letting you ride in the back of the ute or trailer up and down the driveway.

The tip was where a young boy's dreams could come true. You got to feel like a man when you'd throw rubbish on top of a big pile of other rubbish. You would then scan the tip for any signs of something that you could take home with you. Finding bike parts was like finding gold. I found a whole bike once and felt like a millionaire. But as with any great Australian pastime, certain rules need to be followed for it to be done properly.

BILLY'S RULES FOR GOING TO THE TIP

- When you are going to the tip, make a point of announcing it to the whole family. To make sure they hear about it, broadcast it to your mates over the phone. Let them think you're making a real sacrifice. 'Nah, can't go to the races today, mate – I'm going to the tip.' This done, everyone must realise that they have two options: 1) to help, or 2) to stay the hell out of your way.

- On the other hand, try to keep the fact that you're going to the tip hidden from your neighbour. He will try and palm off some of his rubbish on you. Tell him that you have no room for his old lounge suite or broken toilet, let alone that old car body that's been sitting in his backyard.

- You should only consider going to the tip if you have a huge pile of rubbish to get rid of. A boot load isn't enough. Find more. Cut down trees, do what you have to do in order to make a full day of it.

- If you haven't got a trailer, you should borrow or hire one. No-trailer backing experience is necessary – that adds to the fun and adventure of the day. If you're really struggling with the reversing, find a tip where you can just drive straight in without the backing. Try to avoid the shame of having to take the trailer off and walk it in. It doesn't get any more embarrassing than that.

- Plugging in the trailer's lights is optional.

Scenes from the tip: all this great stuff comes under the category of 'general waste' so you really have to fossick around to find what you want. Maybe tips will soon go the way of op shops and get a makeover. They'll set up different departments and you'd have the 'headless mannequin' aisle, the 'useless tyres' aisle and so on. But I guess they'd put the prices up so let's scrap that idea!

- If you own a trailer, never lend it to anyone. I know this rule plays against the previous rule, where I suggest borrowing a trailer, but for some reason a trailer is an Australian bloke's most prized possession. That's right, an oversized wheelbarrow that attaches to your car and is used for carting rubbish means more to a man than his wife and kids.

- When loading the trailer, stack it to the point of overflowing … and then stack it some more. Put garden waste on top. The leaves and branches that fly off on the way to the tip make the drivers behind you keep their distance. Remember, anything that falls off on the way saves you having to unload it when you get there.

- Get a crappy piece of cardboard, write your number plate on it and stick it to the back of the trailer. The harder it is to read, the better.

- Don't use more than two bits of rope to tie down your load. It's just more to untie at the other end. If you don't know how to tie proper knots, don't worry, just tie your normal dodgy knots about eight times, one on top of the other. They shouldn't *all* come undone by the time you get there.

- When you get to the tip, the less information you divulge about your load, the better. Just say 'general waste'. Otherwise they mightn't let you unload. And don't tell them that you've got a boot load as well as the trailer. They'll charge more.

- Use your kids as cheap labour. Keep them motivated with the promise of an ice-cream on the way home.

- Kids often aren't allowed out of the car at the tip but if you can, let them get out and experience the wonderment of chucking rubbish. It cleanses the soul … and the boot.

- When emptying your trailer at the tip, don't just place rubbish on the ground. Make sure you chuck it really hard and watch it smash into a million pieces. Fluorescent light tubes are ideal for this.

- While disposing of your rubbish, never look the bloke next to you in the eye or try to engage him in conversation. It's just like being at the urinal. You're both there to go about your business and that's it.

- While you're unloading your stuff, keep an eye on the tip man to make sure he doesn't see you dumping anything that isn't allowed, e.g. asbestos, toxic waste or a wasp's nest. If you're worried, just throw your stuff on another bloke's pile and play innocent.

- 'One man's trash is another man's treasure' does apply at the tip, so feel free to grab anything you find that may be of value or of use to you. The one rule that applies to this is: 'Don't bring home more than you took to the tip in the first place.'

- On the way home, treat yourself and pop in to the pub for a cool one. If you feel you've worked particularly hard then allow yourself a $10 bet as well.

- When you arrive home, you are to put your feet up and watch telly. You can't be expected to do anything else for a while coz you've just been to the tip. Well done!

Blokes tend to obey most of the rules that I've just mentioned without even thinking about them. They're instinctive. They're part of our make-up as Australian men. But if you ever start doubting yourself, or your wife or kids start questioning your behaviour, then just refer to these rules and all will be sorted. Every man needs to make a trip to the tip on a regular basis to keep himself balanced. Forget about going to yoga, going to the tip can do more for your soul and wellbeing than anything else. So go on, get out there and load your trailer now. You'll feel much better for it.

?

If a deaf person has to go to court is it still called a hearing?

A short history of the wheel

When was the wheel invented? Depends what wheel you're talking about, because I'd say 2000, but I think it was actually in something BC and Pythagoras or someone discovered it, didn't he? Pythagoras comes in handy as a name to roll off the tongue – sounds like you really know the answer.

I can't remember exactly how the wheel came about on the *Footy Show* but it more or less evolved, in the way of all great inventions. Someone came up with the bright idea of taking the wheel to a different local or country footy club every week so they could spin the wheel and win a prize which would be great for the club. All the *Footy Show* needed was some idiot to go far and wide each week, drink beer with the locals and make a fool of himself – enter Anthony William Brownless, former Geelong legend and, at that time, spare parts bloke on the show. I didn't knock it back.

On 23 March 2000, me and the wheel headed for Quantong, which I'd never heard of, just outside Horsham. On the show the week before, I'd said, 'Quantong? I'd rather go to Bali!' so the Quantongians rose to the occasion and had done the place up like it was Bali. They'd brought in sand and had umbrellas everywhere – and it was nothing like Bali! But anyway, we had a big night and that's how the wheel was born.

In 2000 we went to 23 different places including country towns like Terrigal in New South Wales and Karkoo in South Australia and the Garfield Footy Club out Latrobe Valley way, Camperdown down Geelong way, and Goondiwindi in Queensland (home of Gunsynd, the Goondiwindi Grey) and to the Queenscliff Footy Club, known as the Barracoutas (they were struggling and won a car). And we went to Wangaratta Footy Club, where I only recently found out that little Stevie Johnson was sitting in the crowd! He's now a star with the Cats.

Let me tell you, those trips were bloody hard work. I'd rock up, run into some bloke who'd already had a few waiting for me to get there. He'd offer me one through the car window as I pulled up to the ground, and we'd shotgun it coz that's what you do in the country, then we'd have another one while we perused the oval and he told me about all the locals who had played there and how good some of them were. Then I'd go to the club and I'd run into Shifta and Spanna who were on the door, a couple of local legends. I'd have one with Spanna and one with Shifta, and then I'd try to get to the bar but I'd run into two blokes who shoulda been and coulda been the greatest footballers ever … if only. If only one hadn't fallen off the back of a ute one night, spotlighting, and shot his foot off, while the other bloke had cut his foot off helping the old man with the header.

People used to say to me, 'Gee, Billy, you act pissed really well on the wheel.' Let me tell you, I wasn't acting – I'd already have had 5 beers without even getting near the bar.

When I'd finally get to Nackers's Bar – and he'd be a local legend who'd played 600 senior games and 300 in the reserves, who'd been the secretary, the timekeeper and the president of the footy club *and* cooked the hotdogs on Saturday – I'd have a couple with him in the corner. And then the president would come up with his wife, both really excited the wheel had come to town. She'd be all dolled up, hair done beautifully just that day and sporting a new frock from the local hardware shop. So then I'd go over to their table and have a few more beers.

By then, I'd be starting to get a bit tired and emotional and I hadn't even done the segment! But thankfully, Channel Nine would send a producer with me. If you ever watched the wheel on telly, you'd know it only went for about two minutes, but this bloke's real job was to find me and get me up on stage. Because I'd always be a bit disorientated, he'd write the name of the place in texta on a bit of white card so I could tell national television exactly where we were. So eventually I'd get up and tell everyone that if they were quiet they'd get on telly. In those good old days, I'd hear Eddie screaming down the line at me, 'Hurry up Bill, we haven't got much time and we're running late.' So off we'd go, live to air, and as soon as the red light started flashing on the camera and they could see themselves on telly, there'd be the biggest roar – I couldn't hear Ed anymore after that and I'd just run my own little show. Somehow, we'd end up spinning the wheel, and they'd win the car or the really nice crystal (that no-one ever wanted).

But the night didn't end there. Me and half a dozen blokes would be left standing around the bar at 3 am playing every stupid game you play in a country town at that hour. Like how far you can jump forward with both feet together … or you had to guess what sort of alcohol you were drinking out of a brown bag. Then I'd finally get some sleep and wake up in the morning saying, 'That's it, I'm not having a drink next week, it's just too hard!' Then by Saturday I'd be feeling OK, by Tuesday I'd be just about right to go, and by Thursday, back on it.

I loved it. At every club I went to I'd meet a legend, or two or five. They were all very good to me because it was like Santa Claus coming to town. And it was very good for the clubs because they'd run a raffle at $5 ticket to see who'd get to spin the wheel and be in the spotlight on telly, so they'd raise a bit of money. They'd sell out of hamburgers and hotdogs, and would run out of grog at most joints, having to get extra supplies from the local pub. You'd hear people saying things like, 'This is the best night we've ever had for our town.'

But it wasn't great for me and the kidneys. It's exhausting having a drink with almost everyone in a town.

The Wheel – 2000

23 March	Quantong	VIC
30 March	Goolwa	SA
6 April	Apsley	VIC
13 April	Cockatoo/Gembrook	VIC
20 April	Keilor	VIC
27 April	Terrigal/Avoca Football Club	NSW
4 May	Donald Football Club	VIC
11 May	Yallourn North Football Club	VIC
17 May	Karkoo	SA
25 May	Melton Central	VIC
1 June	Mitcham Football Club	VIC
8 June	Sydenham Football Club	VIC
15 June	Montrose	VIC
22 June	Garfield	VIC
29 June	North Dandenong	VIC
6 July	Glenroy	VIC
13 July	Camperdown	VIC
20 July	Queenscliff	VIC
27 July	Belgrave	VIC
5 August	Wangaratta	VIC
10 August	Crib Point	VIC
17 August	Goondiwindi	QLD
24 August	Melbourne Uni	VIC

LOUNGE SUIT

Every bloke must have at least one suit. If you've got two, consider yourself a high flyer. You can't avoid dressing up for a wedding. All the other blokes will be in a suit so it's a good idea to wear the same, otherwise you'll stick out like the fat bridesmaid. Suits pretty much look alike so it's all about the shirt, tie and shoes. But a great suit, shirt and tie can be completely ruined by a pair of dodgy shoes – they need to be sleek, sharp and shiny. Your old school shoes just won't cut it. A wedding invitation actually tells you what to wear so it's pretty hard to stuff up.

DRESS TO IMPRESS

Especially the first few visits. In fact, wait a good twelve months before you start wearing tracksuits. You have no choice. You're already starting on the back foot. They're worried that you're not good enough for their daughter. So if you try to dress good enough, you'll be tipping the scales back in your favour. Do whatever you can to wear clothing that covers your tattoos and/or scars you received from your time in prison.

CASUAL

Don't be too well dressed because no-one will give you a good deal or a discount. On the other hand, don't dress too poorly because you'll be stopped every time you leave a shop to have your bags checked. The biggest mistake I make is wearing thongs when I'm going to buy shoes. If you want to try on shoes they give you socks to wear from a box behind the counter. How many other blokes have put these socks on before me? 20? 50? 150? The key to shopping is dressing comfortably. You're going to be doing a lot of walking around, so wear runners. Or if I go shopping with the Darl – hiking boots, a backpack and a tent.

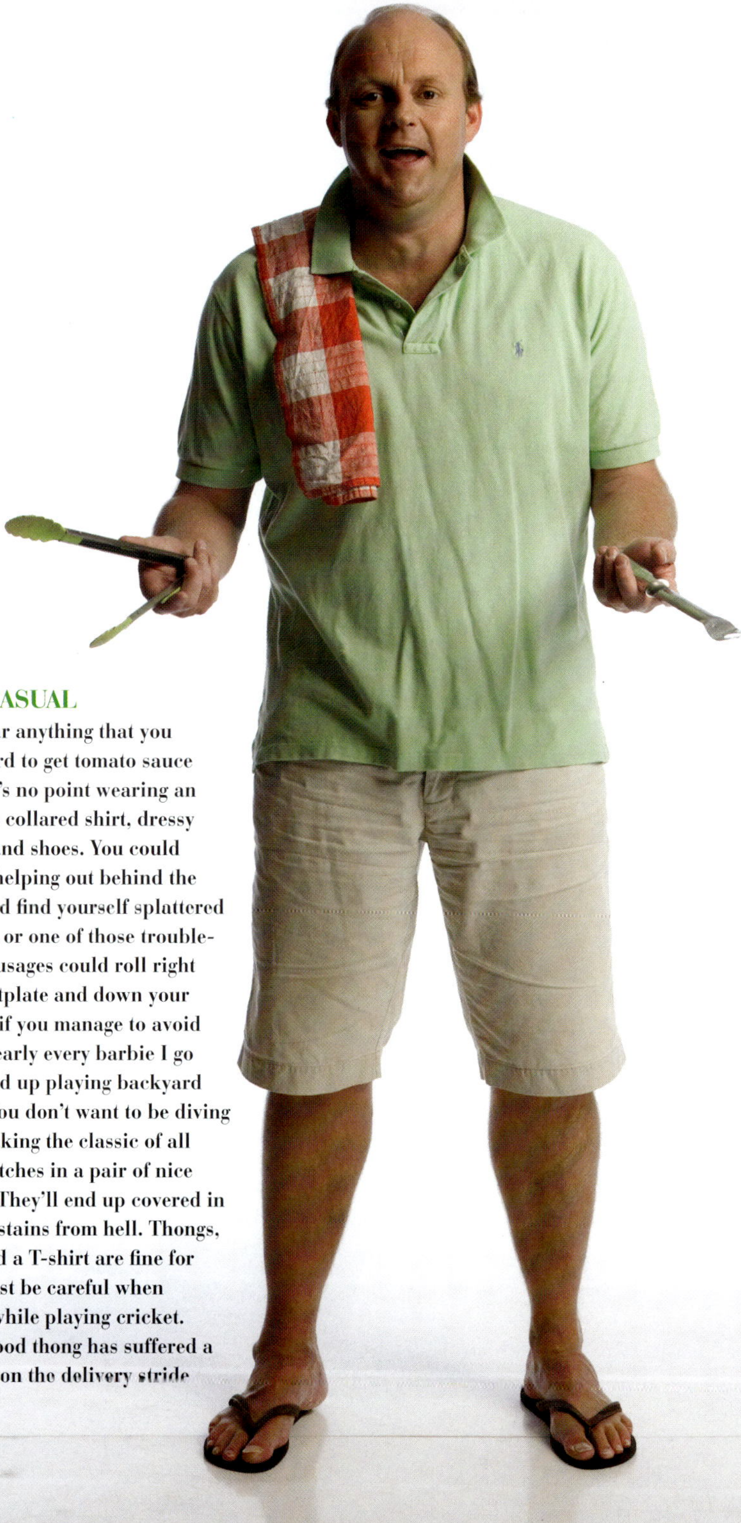

VERY CASUAL

Don't wear anything that you can't afford to get tomato sauce on. There's no point wearing an expensive collared shirt, dressy trousers and shoes. You could be stuck helping out behind the barbie and find yourself splattered in grease, or one of those trouble-maker sausages could roll right off the hotplate and down your leg. Even if you manage to avoid that, at nearly every barbie I go to, you end up playing backyard cricket. You don't want to be diving around taking the classic of all classic catches in a pair of nice trousers. They'll end up covered in the grass stains from hell. Thongs, shorts and a T-shirt are fine for a BBQ. Just be careful when bowling while playing cricket. Many a good thong has suffered a blow out on the delivery stride

NO SPEEDOS!

You need to have the body of a male model to wear budgie smugglers. If you own any other type of body then your imperfections will be magnified by 100 in those things. As far as I'm concerned, boardies or footy shorts are the only acceptable items for blokes to wear at the beach. If you're very pale then wear a T-shirt as well. Not just for your protection, but because a hairy, chubby, pale-skinned man is not good for anyone to be looking at. If you've got man-boobs don't let your T-shirt get wet. It will give other blokes near you a weird sense of confusion.

SLOPPY

Whether you're taking them to school or to a party, wear old, disgusting clothes and threaten that you'll get out of the car when you drop them off. Wearing white socks with thongs is one of my favourites. There's no good reason for doing this other than for you to have a bit of fun as a parent. You run around all the time for your kids, so you should be allowed to enjoy yourself once in a while. You deserve it.

YOUR CHOICE

It's your house. You can wear whatever you bloody well like. You don't have to wear anything at all. Just check how much the neighbours can see in first. If you don't like them very much, try mowing the lawn naked. That'll freak them out. The more daring among us will sometimes BBQ in the nude. I don't recommend it. You wouldn't want to prick the wrong sausage with the fork.

A NOTE ON LYCRA

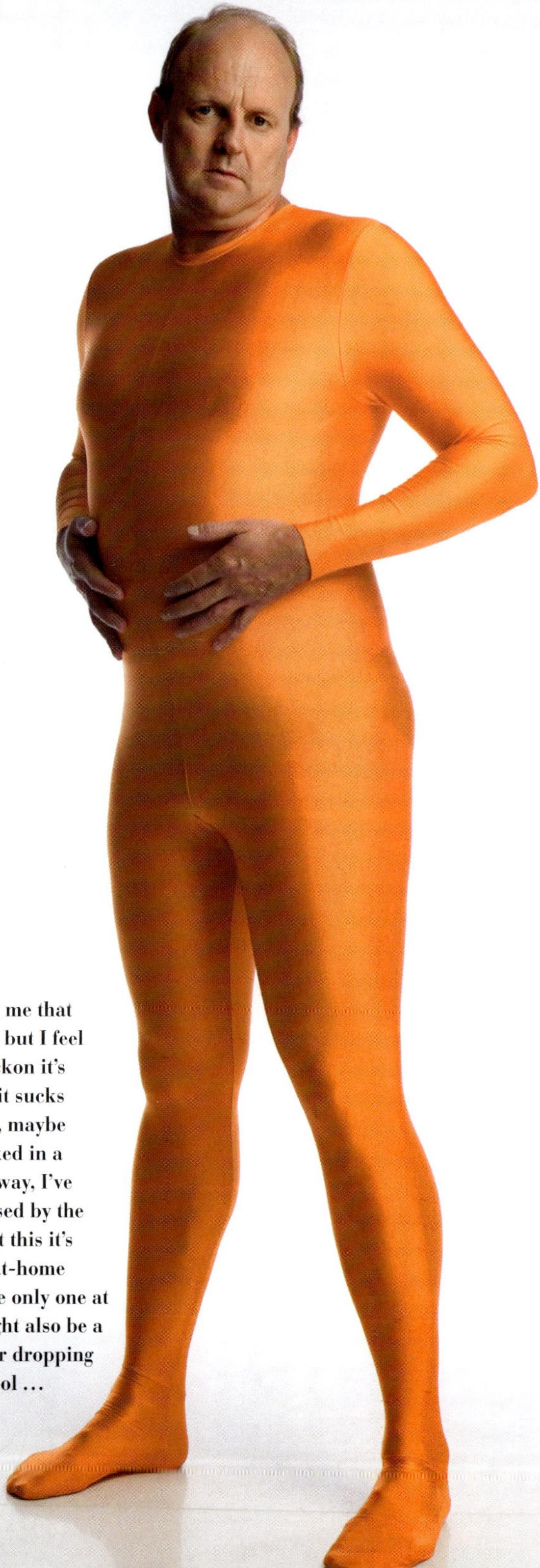

SEXY

No one agrees with me that I look good in this, but I feel fantastic in it. I reckon it's slimming because it sucks everything in (well, maybe some bits gets sucked in a bit too much). Anyway, I've recently been advised by the Fashion Police that this it's probably best for at-home wear. When I'm the only one at home. Hmmm, might also be a good alternative for dropping the kids off at school ...

The wheel was back in 2001, and again we visited 23 clubs. The club rooms of Catani Football Club down near Cranbourne had been burnt down so we went there first, and they actually won the car that night. We went to Yarrambat Footy Club; they had a weightlifter who was training for the Olympics, so we set up a swing thing where he'd lift me. Worked beautifully the three times we practised it but as soon as we did it live to air, I fell off the swing and skinned my arm. The show went on though – luckily I was fairly anaesthetised by that stage.

We took the wheel to the Holden assembly plant in Elizabeth, South Australia and Peter Brock was there; the wheel was sponsored by Holden that year. Another highlight was going to Leeton, up in the bush in New South Wales. I still remember getting back to some bloke's house at 3 am – we'd had a few frothies by that stage. He got his missus out of bed, and she cooked up the best seafood basket I've ever had. She had the deep fried fish, the calamari, the dim sims, the chips, all piled up, and we sat there like kings. It was fantastic.

We went to Kangaroo Island – it's only a little island but it's got four footy teams and we had a great night there. We went to a couple of places in Tassie but Motton Preston sticks in my mind. The natives were very friendly but honestly, if you ran off the road there they wouldn't find you for five years. And we took the great Bobby 'fair dinkum unbelievable' Davis back to his hometown of Clunes. That was another great night.

At the end of 2001, I think they thought the wheel had run its race. It was getting pretty expensive travelling interstate. The wheel itself was pretty big and had to be transported by

The Wheel – 2001

22 March	Catani	VIC
5 April	Yarroweyah	VIC
11 April	Deep Creek	SA
18 April	Sylvan Football Club	QLD
26 April	Chelsea Heights Football Club	VIC
3 May	Waverley Blues	VIC
10 May	Melton Juniors Football Club	VIC
17 May	Box Hill	VIC
24 May	Yarrambat Football Club	VIC
31 May	Panton Hill	VIC
7 June	Holden Assembly Plant, Elizabeth	SA
14 June	Eastern Lions Junior FC	VIC
5 July	Leeton Whitton	NSW
12 July	Kingscote FC, Kangaroo Island	SA
19 July	Huonville	TAS
26 July	Bell Post Hill Football Club	VIC
2 August	Motton Preston Football Club	TAS
9 August	South Belgrave Football Club	VIC
16 August	Clunes Football Club	VIC
23 August	Friends Old Boys Football Club	TAS
30 August	Leopold Football Club	VIC
6 September	Wyndham Vale Football Club	VIC
14 September	Boronia Football Club	VIC

truck to all those places and the costs of doing the live feed were adding up. And maybe they were worried about whether I could keep up the pace – I certainly was! So me and the wheel had a bit of a spell.

Then, after six years, the wheel came out of retirement in 2007, but we only made five trips, every 4 or so weeks. We went to Barnawartha first, a little town struggling because of the drought. A kid called Dawson Simpson had won the raffle to spin the wheel – they won $10 000 on 22 March. Then, believe it or not, at the end of that year, young Dawson was drafted to Geelong and he wears number 16, my old number.

We went to Tyabb and had a yabbie race; did a bit of sheep shearing at Wunghnu in the Goulburn Valley, and had a dim sim eating competition in Langwarrin – I got beaten by this big fat bloke. Then in August, the last one for 2007, we went to Ararat Footy Club where I had a bike race with a kid who I reckon is on the way to being a very good cyclist. I wore the now-famous orange lycra suit – I thought I looked magnificent. We did the live-to-air and they won the Dodge. Then after a few frothies, the suit felt so good (and it was a bit cold that night) I left it on all the way back to Melbourne in the car. I have a bloke who drives me because I'm often a tad under the weather coming back from a wheel segment. We had to stop at the Shell servo under the Westgate Bridge and my mate put the petrol in and I went in and paid. The man behind the jump didn't even raise an eyebrow as I walked through in head-to-toe orange lycra!

?

Why are 'semi' trailers bigger than normal trucks?

In 2008, I milked the cows in Lockington, also drought-stricken, and I reckon the whole town was there in the football and netball club rooms. Then we went to Warragul and gave the ferrets a run, literally. That night I also had a little episode where my front tooth fell out on TV. Garry Lyon thought it was the funniest thing he'd ever seen so they replayed it again while I was there. And then in June I gave the orange lycra another run, this time to the Richmond Central footy club. Any excuse!

So far, 54 different football and netball clubs across Australia have done really well out of the wheel – isn't that fantastic?

The Wheel – 2007

22 March	Barnawartha Football Club	VIC
3 May	Tyabb Football Club	VIC
17 May	Wunghnu Football Club	VIC
14 June	Langwarrin Football Club	VIC
11 August	Ararat Football Club	VIC

The Wheel – 2008 (so far)

17 April	Lockington Football Club	VIC
8 May	Warragul Football Club	VIC
5 June	Richmond Central Football Club	VIC

?

Why do they call them 'apartments' when they are all stuck together?

Rules for backyard cricket

Backyard cricket has been played in Australia for over a hundred years. In that time it has given birth to similar versions played in driveways, hallways, lounge rooms, classrooms and even the office. It's got to the point where you don't even need a proper bat and ball anymore. A ruler and a piece of screwed up paper will do. When I was a boy, for me and my mates backyard cricket was the only chance we got to play on turf. Not good turf, mind you. In backyard cricket it's usually a crappy, bumpy strip, with a dog poo sitting halfway down the wicket. The only way it qualifies as a cricket pitch is because that morning, you mowed it to be a bit shorter than the rest of the backyard.

Our backyard in Jerilderie was bigger than your average suburban one. We basically had two blocks. One block had the house on it and the other block had the cricket pitch on it. That block was as sacred as the MCG. Pitch invaders were shown no mercy. Once Mum decided to venture onto it and my two brothers tackled her to the ground and escorted her off like two policeman with a streaker. We took great pride in our turf wicket. We didn't have a roller, so we'd sit bricks on it to flatten it.

Dad saw how much me and my brothers loved playing cricket, so one day he decided he was going to make us boys a concrete pitch. His first effort wasn't bad, just a bit short. It was only 5 metres long. Still, pretty good for Dad. He wasn't known as a handyman. He said, 'Don't worry boys, I'll extend it.' And he did. He put another 5 metres on. Would have been handy if the new 5 metre bit had been in line with the old 5 metres. It wasn't just out – it was out by a fair bit. As far as I know, it's the only boomerang shaped cricket pitch in existence. But a very versatile pitch. You could play any form of the game on it: Test match or one-dayer. And it was playable in all conditions: rain, hail or shine. Just not good on the elbows when you were sliding head first into the crease.

A tennis ball was OK on a concrete pitch but we preferred to use a 'compo ball'. The compo ball was the cheapest and deadliest cricket ball ever made. It looked like a real cricket ball from a distance but instead of having a leather covering, it had a hard rubberised one, complete with replica cricket ball stitches. Boy could that compo ball swing. And great for bowling bouncers that could kill a man or at least take his head off. You don't see many compo balls these days. I wouldn't be surprised if they've been outlawed. If anyone can get hold of a new one, I'd be happy to pay big bucks for it, no questions asked.

The biggest thrill for us boys was when it came to buying our cricket gear. We didn't have a sports store near us, so we had to order our cricket gear from The Greg Chappell Cricket Centre and then wait for it to arrive. That wait felt like forever and, I can tell you, opening that package on the day it arrived was like discovering Dad's secret coin drawer. It was bigger than Christmas day. We were even more excited at the thought that maybe the great man, Greg Chappell, had packed it himself.

The game of backyard cricket has heaps of rules that are now part of the Australian way of life. Most people follow them closely but a lot of backyards have their own house rules as well. Often they are made up on the spot. Being the oldest brother meant that I would make up any rules that suited me at the time. Which would lead to the most common way a game of Brownless backyard cricket was abandoned – one of my little brothers cracking the sads and sooking off. Looking back, it would have been handy to have had an official list of rules to refer to. That's why I've tried to put one together here. If anyone wants to argue the point just pull out this book or, even better, suggest they buy it. Before we get into it, the most important rule to remember is that everyone at your house, no matter what age, gender or skill level, should be allowed to play without fear of being hurt. Unless, of course, it's mainly your mates there, in which case you're playing for sheep stations. You bowl full pelt, appeal everything, get in the batsman's face and no kids or women are allowed.

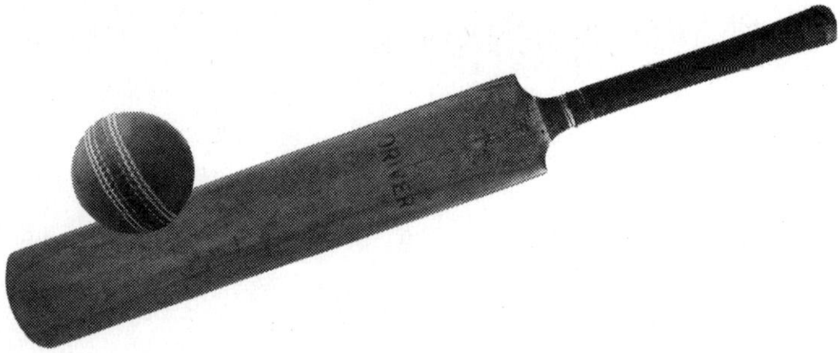

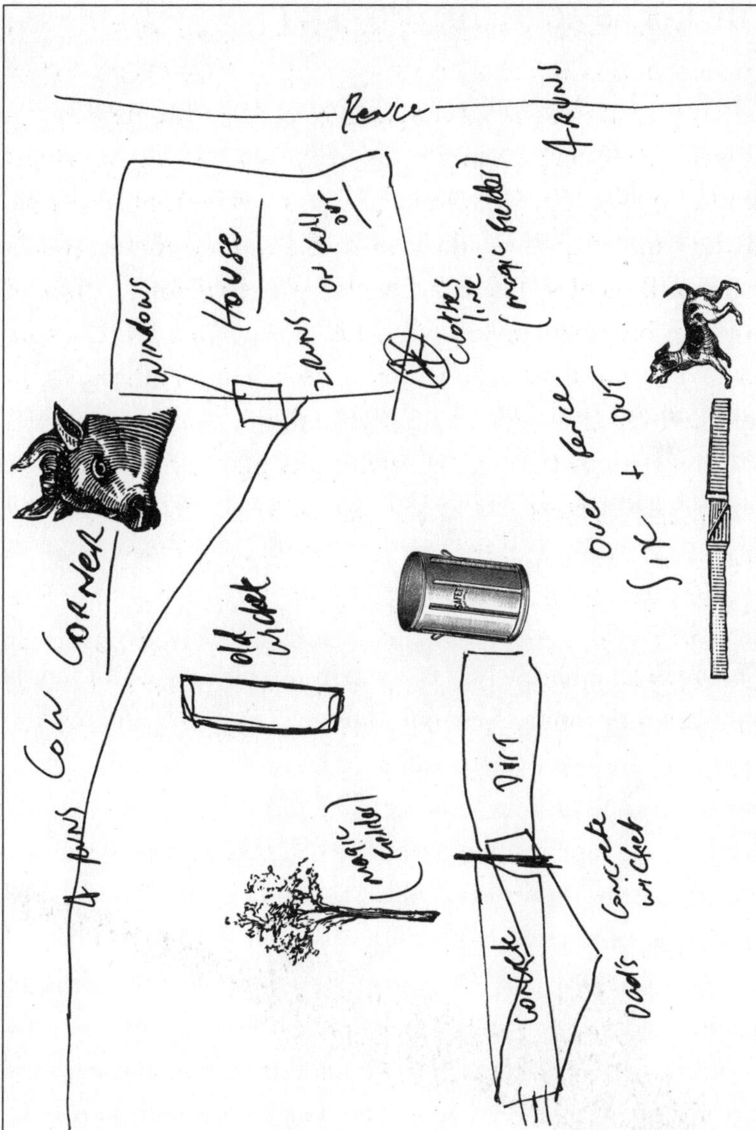

The pitch at No. 1 Coreen Street, Jerilderie, New South Wales

THE RULES ACCORDING TO BILLY

The toss: The toss is to be conducted by spinning a bat in the air. One of the captains calls 'hills' or 'valleys' (also known as 'roofs' or 'flats'). If the bat lands with the back of the bat facing up, then that is 'hills'. If the flat face is showing, that is 'valleys'. If you win the toss, always bowl. It's important to get first use of the new ball on a, more often than not, dodgy wicket.

Can't go out first ball: A batsman cannot be out on the first ball he faces. This is a good rule as it sets the tone by saying that the game is not to be taken too seriously. If that batsman goes on to make 100, feel free to remind him not to enjoy it because technically, he was out first ball.

The ball: The tennis ball is the ball of choice. An old tennis ball, not a new one. New ones bounce too much and are too expensive to lose over the fence. The ball can be taped with electrical tape to help it swing. The tape can't be re-applied until the old tape completely comes off. Hiding washers under the taping to obtain even more swing is unacceptable. For added pace you can wet the tennis ball but this is only allowed to be done once per batsman. The traditional 'bowling of a lemon, orange or apple instead of the ball' joke is only permitted once per game. Some money-hungry manufacturers have jumped on the backyard cricket bandwagon and have brought out balls like 'The Swingking', specifically designed for backyard cricket. Personally, I don't like 'em. I'm yet to be convinced that anything plays as well as the taped tennis ball.

The bowler: The bowler is to bowl as many balls as he likes until someone asks him how many balls he has left, to which he replies, 'One left!' The bowler will generally come off a shortened run, unless the previous ball was smashed over his head, in which case he has to retrieve the ball and may start a long, angry run-up from the point where he picked up the ball.

Wides: Have to be really obvious and need more than just the batsman to call them. A wide may or may not be bowled again depending on the house rules and may or may not score a run. Wides will come more into play towards the end of a close match, in which case they must be rebowled.

The stumps: A rubbish bin is to be used as the stumps. The tennis ball thumping into an old metal bin used to make a great sound when someone was bowled, especially if the lid came off as well. Much controversy erupted with the introduction of the wheelie bin. The wickets were so much taller now, giving the bowler more to aim at. Scores began to drop and me and my mates considered dumping our old batting records and starting all over again. Other acceptable wickets include an esky, a cardboard box, a boogie board or a chair.

The wicket keeper: If there are a small number of players then you can have 'automatic wickie'. In this case there is no wicket keeper and any snick behind is automatically out. If you do have a wicket keeper he is permitted to use just one hand if he is holding a stubbie in the other. The wicket keeper can also take the ball and kick the bin at the same time to try and trick the batsman into thinking he has been bowled. Another wicket keeper trick is to move the wickets a bit wider of the batsman. The bowler then aims the ball at the new position and bowls the unsuspecting batsman out. Watch the wicket keeper closely. A lazy fielder might try and spend the whole afternoon behind the stumps.

LBW: No LBW in backyard cricket. Too hard to judge. Especially after a few stubbies (unless you have your own 'hawkeye' installed at home).

Tippetty run: Tippetty run is optional. It refers to a variation of the game where the batsman must run if he hits the ball. It really keeps the game moving and rotates the strike but you may get sick of the following argument: 'You hit that!' 'No I didn't!' 'Yes you did' 'I didn't!' 'You bloody well did!' 'Nah, it came off my leg! And so on.

Six and out: Hitting the ball over the fence is six and out. The batsman has to jump the fence and get the ball himself, no matter how vicious the dog or the neighbour is. If the batsman has difficulty finding the ball then other fielders can jump the fence and help. The length of the search depends on how many spare tennis balls there are or how vicious the dog and/or neighbour is. Hitting the house on the full can also be out.

Lost ball: If a batsman hits the ball into an area where the fielders can't find it (like a thick bush) the batsmen may be called over to help find it. A fielder may pretend he can't find the ball in the hope that the batsman will go for an extra run. When this occurs, the fielder will pick the ball up straight away and try and run the batsman out.

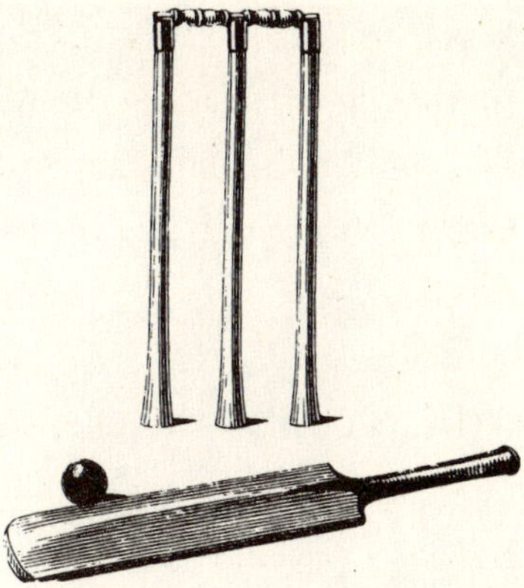

One hand, one bounce: A player is able to catch the batsman out with one hand as long as the ball has bounced only once, hence the name 'one hand, one bounce'. Personally, I hate this rule but I had to include it because it is so widely used. As far as I'm concerned, if you hit the ball into the ground first, then that's a good shot and doesn't deserve to get you out. The variation on this rule, which I prefer, is when a player is out if caught one-handed after the ball has bounced off an obstacle such as a house, garage, car or window (often referred to as 'one hand off the roof').

Any wicket: Fielders can run the batsman out by hitting either wicket, regardless of which end the batsman is running to.

Safe: If there is only one batsman and he makes a single or a three and ends up stranded at the non-striker's end, then he must yell, 'Safe!', 'Wicket!' or 'wicket leave!' before walking back to the batting crease, otherwise he may be run out.

Magic fielders: Similar to the automatic wicket keeper rule, magic fielders can range from a tree to a clothesline or a chair to a BBQ. The batsman is out if he hits any magic fielder on the full.

Is that really me?

The clothesline rule: If Mum has just put a load of washing on the line then there's a good chance that the game will be postponed. If Mum leaves the house at any stage and is going to be out for a while then the game may recommence.

Catcher bats next: Whoever catches, bowls or runs out the batsman gets to bat next. This rule doesn't really give everyone a go and can result in an uneven game. More popular with beach cricket.

Walking: Never, ever walk (sorry Gilly). Even if the bowler, keeper and all the other fielders claim you nicked it, always stand your ground. Wait for an independent observer (like a parent or a neighbour sticking his head over the fence) to verify that you are out before you even think about walking. At this stage, still argue the point before storming off and throwing the bat into something that makes a loud noise, like the shed.

Creases: The bowling crease is around about where the wickets at the bowler's end are. The batsman's crease is to be roughly judged by the batsman, who measures it by using the length of the bat plus the handle. He then marks it by dragging his bat back and forth on the ground. Not sure if this is the official measurement as I am yet to see Ricky Ponting do it.

Scoring: Scores are to be kept in players' heads. Don't just leave it up to the batsman. If he's the only one keeping score, then he will reach 50 in no time. Runs are to be determined according to the layout of the backyard and how close obstacles are to the batsman. One fence may be worth four runs but a closer fence may only be worth two runs. This also allows for special shots, e.g. if you hit the ball and it lands in the wheelbarrow then it's worth ten runs.

You bat you field: If you've had a bat, you can't go back inside until you've fielded while everyone else has a bat. Some fathers let their little sons get away with quitting after they've had a bat. That's teaching them a bad habit that could end up turning the kid into a bit of a wussy boy.

Old man tweakers: At any time the game may be interrupted by an old man who wanders out to roll the arm over. After he bowls about four or five deliveries and gets absolutely no turn (except for one, which hits a bump but he still claims was all him), he's normally had enough and goes back inside. Getting out to this bowler is the most embarrassing way to be dismissed in backyard cricket.

Last man gets his tucker: The last batsman for each team is allowed to bat without a partner. Even if you have always played this rule, that doesn't stop everyone yelling out 'Last man gets his tucker!' It's just one of those phrases that feels really good to say.

?

Why do we say 'bye, bye' but not 'hi, hi'?

These rules alone won't make for a top game of backyard cricket. It's up to the group playing to establish their own code of conduct (refer to Australia v India games). Impersonations are also strongly encouraged. Seeing a mate running in to bowl doing a Maxie Walker impression is enough to put you off to the point where you'll play a poor shot and get bowled. Other well used take-offs include Dennis Lillee, Jeff Thomson, Bob Willis, Michael Holding (not an easy one), Richard Hadlee, Kerry O'Keefe and Lenny Pascoe. Anyone with a suspect bowling action is to be dubbed 'Murali' and everyone else is to yell 'No ball!' as he bowls.

I hope these rules can be of some use but I'd still suggest that you hang on to the tried and tested underhanded cheating that has done so well for you over the years. Warning: these rules are not approved by the ICC. Happy cricketing!

The mad professor at work.

More wisdom from Blighty

Malcolm Blight is an Adelaide boy. Well, an Adelaide legend. Actually he's more of an icon now. He was a gun footballer, for starters. One of the best the game has seen. Silky smooth skills on both sides of the body, could take a specky and kick the ball a mile. After dominating in Adelaide, where he topped the goal kicking and won a Magarey Medal, he was soon snapped up by North Melbourne. His time there truly showed just what a class act he was. He won a Brownlow and a couple of flags. He represented both Victoria and South Australia. He was an out-and-out champion. He did it all. Was there anything left for him to prove?

Well, in 1990 he was coaching us for the first time against Adelaide in Adelaide. He was coming back to his home town, in front of a packed house at Football Park. Despite everything he had achieved in his career, you could see that he was getting tense and feeling the pressure of this game. He was on edge, alright. He wanted to impress his fellow Adelaidians. He still had something to prove.

I'm in the middle of doing a bit of pre-game stretching, while at the same time watching Blighty pace up and down the change room. Today's game is playing on his mind. I can understand why he would be a tad nervous. The people of Adelaide absolutely love him. They think the sun shines out of his backside, which I suppose, makes him feel even more pressure to perform. I'm thinking to myself, once we get out there and get into the game, he'll probably start to settle down and we'll be back into our normal routine.

The call comes for us to get ready to run out onto the ground. It surprises me coz it's about 10 minutes earlier than we usually get out there. Maybe we're doing an extended warm-up or maybe the game could be starting at a different time for TV reasons. Whatever the case, we're down the race and out onto the ground to the thunderous silence of the Adelaide crowd.

We start our warm-up drills and I must admit, I'm feeling in pretty good touch, as are the rest of the boys. Not many balls hit the turf and we're doing it at a cracking pace. We get into a tight little handball exercise and I can tell by looking around at my team-mates that we're all starting to get a bit concerned that there is no opposition yet. Adelaide are still in their rooms. It looks like we've come out way too early. Why would Blighty have done that?

With our warm-up complete, Buddha gathers us all in and says, 'Boys, follow me.' We run off in a group, heading towards the Adelaide race. We get to the race and stop. It's at this point that I'm starting to worry. 'Alright, boys,' he says, 'we have to split up into two groups of ten. Each group of ten is to form a line on either side of the Adelaide race.' OK, now I'm really worried. Blighty's obviously put a bit of thought into this, which can only mean bad things for us and I, for one, am dreading the next instruction. Buddha goes on, 'Now, when the Adelaide boys come out, we have to clap them onto the ground.' Here we are in front of 50 000 'lovely' Adelaide home fans, on national television I might add, and we're lined up like Little Leaguers waiting for the big blokes to run out. I've been humiliated on a football field heaps of times but never before the game has started. What really gets me is that I can't believe Buddha has agreed and allowed this to happen. To Buddha's credit, though, he did insist that if Blighty expects all of us to line up, then he can line up too. Sure enough, Blighty jogs over and joins one of the lines.

The crowd around the race start cheering. This can only mean one thing – the Adelaide boys are on the way out. We start clapping. They're being led out by their captain, Chris McDermott, who is basically a chunk of concrete with legs. He can't believe what he is seeing. This big smile comes across his face. Which is rare for him. He only ever smiles like that when he's looking down at you lying helplessly on the ground, after he's just poleaxed you. And boy is he giving us a face-full as he jogs past. As are his team-mates. They are getting stuck in to us big time. The last player out is Nigel Smart, who takes his time to run past each and every Geelong player and give them an individual pasting, the likes of which I've never witnessed on a football field before. It's one of the most degrading and embarrassing experiences of my life. I just want the ground to open up and swallow me whole. The Adelaide crowd are loving it. Like they need any more ammunition to abuse us with.

What was Blighty's reason for doing this, you might ask? As we finish clapping, he tells us, 'reverse psychology, boys.

It's a powerful tool. They've run out and just seen you blokes clapping them onto their own ground, so they're already thinking to themselves, "These blokes aren't fair dinkum. They haven't come here to play. This will be a walk in the park for us."' Blighty has a sly grin on his face. 'That'll play right into our hands, boys. Now, get out there and do your stuff. They won't know what's hit them.'

The game starts and we go bang, bang, and kick the first two goals within a couple of minutes. I'm thinking, how good's this, Blighty's a genius. This is sensational, we've caught them completely off guard. They're dumbfounded. Our little stunt has really thrown them. We go on to lose the game by 58 points.

I caught up with Malcolm recently, over a few beers, and I was recounting the story to him. He refused to admit that he got it wrong. He still claims that it was the best loss we ever had against them.

I'd probably just kicked another lazy ten.

How to remember names

Most people would admit that they're not very good at remembering names. Faces are a lot easier to remember. Sometimes you see a familiar face but can't remember the name or where you know them from. Here's an example of this very situation occurring. It involves me, and – this will surprise you – I wasn't the one stuffing up the name. I was, in actual fact, the victim. Don't worry, I have embarrassed myself heaps of times by getting names and faces wrong but I'd rather tell this story this time.

In 1996, I was in Noosa with the family for a bit of a holiday. Lucy was about two and Nicky was pregnant with Ruby. It was good to get away for a while and we had some magnificent weather. If you've been to Noosa, you'll know what a relaxing place it can be. Our hotel was pretty busy while we were there because it was hosting a doctors' conference. There were doctors everywhere which made it very handy if there was a medical emergency. Thankfully, there wasn't. The only pain I experienced on the trip was when I did a belly whacker in the pool.

Noosa is the kind of place where you just say hi to other people you see walking around. One morning we were in the hotel foyer when this bloke, his wife and two daughters walked in. We did the polite thing and said hi. They said hi back. We ran into them a few mornings in a row and talked a little bit more each time. There was one day when we all stopped and had an even bigger conversation. There was some general chit chat about the weather and stuff. Lovely people they were. We were chatting for a good 5 minutes when the bloke cuts in and decides to introduce his family to me. He starts with his wife and goes, 'Julie, this is Dr Col Robertson. These are my daughters, Stephanie and Amanda, this is Dr Col Robertson.' Nicky and I have given each other a puzzled look. This bloke has mistaken me for, of all things, a doctor! A butcher, maybe – but a doctor? The problem now was that we'd been talking for so long that it felt too late to tell him he was wrong, so I just went with it. I could be Dr Col Robertson for 5 minutes. No-one's going to get hurt. Then I thought to myself, I can't introduce Nicky and Lucy coz I don't know who they're supposed to be. I brought the conversation to an end and we did the only thing we thought was right – we took off as fast as we could, giggling all the way. Of course, we spent the rest of the trip bumping into him every day. He'd wave and go, 'G'day, Col.' I'd wave back and say, 'G'day, mate.' When we were leaving Noosa, I made a point of saying goodbye to him. This was my chance to finally tell him the truth. It wasn't going to be easy, so I piked out and told him that I had to rush back to perform some emergency surgery.

On returning home, I did some research and found out that Dr Colin Robertson does exist. He is the director

Why do people duck in the rain? Do they think it won't hit them?

of respiratory medicine at the Royal Children's Hospital in Melbourne; he's an expert on asthma. He will have some explaining to do, though, coz when I was in Noosa, I was telling everyone I was a gynaecologist. While writing this book, I did ring Dr Colin Robertson and he was amused by the story. When I asked how many times he's been mistaken for me, he said, 'None'. Then again, he is usually in a hospital, dressed like a doctor and treating asthma patients, so not much chance of people thinking it's me.

It is a relief to know that I'm not the only person who doesn't remember who people are. In most cases I can cleverly cover myself by just calling people 'Nackers' or 'Cocko'. Feel free to use those words if they will help you out, depending on the situation, of course. If you're meeting public figures or important people, like the Queen – I wouldn't use them. ('That woman over there, in the crown and eating all the sandwiches – what's her name again?') Anyway, if you're forgetting who the Queen is, your problem's much bigger than you first thought.

Don't show that you have no idea who they are.

Smile like you know them: 'G'day Cocko!'

I suppose we feel bad about forgetting people's names because we know how deflating it is when someone forgets ours. Our name is what identifies us. If someone forgets it then it's like that person doesn't rate you. But we do it to others all the time. The worst is when you meet someone for the first time and as soon as you swap names and shake hands, their name has gone straight out of your head. You kick yourself and promise that you won't do that again but you never do anything differently next time.

The 'Nackers' and 'Cocko' approach is only a band-aid solution to the problem but there are other tips and strategies that can help you remember people's names. I've tried some of them and they actually do work. That's not an airtight guarantee, by the way. So don't try and get your money back on this book if they don't work. A lot of the things I'm about to tell you may seem like common sense but they obviously need to be put out there. If I can help one bloke remember a name then I've made a difference. OK, here we go. Read on if you want to become a new name remembering freak.

Before you walk into a party or a function, stop thinking about how you look or if your car will be OK where you parked it or when was the last time you washed the shirt you're wearing. Instead, make the decision to concentrate when people are being introduced to you. If you don't hear their name properly, ask them to repeat it. If it's an unusual name, ask them to spell it. Whatever you do, don't laugh at a funny sounding name. It will offend the person more than forgetting it would. I won't be doing that again. It's not like I'd never heard the name 'Ophelia' before. People are very sensitive about their names, so there are a lot of comments you should avoid. For example, never do what I once did and tell the person about a pet with the same name as theirs. ('My cousin's got a dog called Jessie.')

I find that one of the best things to do is to look a person in the eye when you meet them and then repeat their name straight away. 'Nice to meet you, Kevin.' If you throw their name into the conversation, that'll help too. 'So, Kevin, do you prefer salt and vinegar or BBQ flavoured chips?' (This is an example. Not a recommended conversation starter. Although, I did once have a frank and open 45 minute discussion on chip flavours with Buddha Hocking. He prefers chicken flavour.)

Another good technique is to think of another word that describes the person and starts with the same letter as the person's name, e.g. 'Tall Tim', 'Greedy Graham', 'Annoying Anita' or 'Boring Barry'. I met them all at a party once. Left early that night, right after Creepy Cathy and Sleazy Steve cornered us. With this one, be careful not to say any of these out loud. Makes me wonder what someone would come up with for me? 'Brilliant Billy', maybe … or 'Boyish Good Looks Billy'? Suffice to say, this method works – how do you think Big Bad Bustling Barry Hall got his nickname?

If you have forgotten someone's name and have been chatting for far too long to ask them again then a good trick is to excuse yourself, go to the bar and tell someone you know to come over and introduce themselves to this person. That way you get to hear their name again. It just goes to show, those people who have parties where they get everyone to wear name tags are really onto something. No, hang on, I take that back. I can't possibly endorse a name tag wearing party.

?

Why is it OK to be a 'wise man' but not a 'wise guy'?

The most common way we get caught out with names is if we see someone we haven't seen for a long time or we see someone out of the environment we're used to seeing them in. In these situations it's always a lot harder to put a name to a face. A good thing to do here is to start asking them questions that will help trigger a memory which, in turn, will cough up their name. Questions like, 'How's work going?' or 'How's the family?' or 'When was the last time we saw each other?' or 'Is that your real hair?' This should give you something to build on.

It's a real bonus if you're with your partner coz then you can run through the names before you go into a party. I do it with Nicky all the time. 'So, let's see if I've got this right. Dave's married to Cath, Craig's married to Kerry and Phil was married to Cath but he ran off with her sister, yeah? And your name is Nicky, yeah?'

Remembering someone's name shows you care. In business, it shows that you're professional. Hopefully, you now have some strategies to arm yourself with. But sometimes, the best laid plans can fall over. Remembering names doesn't come easy. You need to apply yourself. When one strategy doesn't work, try another. If you're still getting nowhere and all else fails, then I have two words for you, my friend – 'Nackers' and 'Cocko'.

Billy rates takeaway

Home-cooked meals are the best, without doubt. There' is something special about having put a meal together using your own skill and kitchen appliances. Nicky can do it standing on her head. If I manage to get a meal right, it's a bloody miracle. My problem is that I don't follow recipes too closely. I'm a rebel in the kitchen. I like to do things my own way and cook with a bit of flair. I'm a renegade. I mix things up a bit by adding my own ingredients. Some weird-looking meals come out of the oven and people look at them and say, 'What's that called?' My response: 'Does it matter? Do you need to label my creations? You can't put a tag on genius.' Every now and again I somehow pull it off and boy, do I let everyone know about it! There is no better feeling in this world than when all of the planets in the kitchen align and you have the spuds, the cauliflower and the meat all cooked and ready to serve at exactly the same time.

In this day and age, with our busy lifestyles and with both partners often working full-time, it's impossible to cook every night of the week. That's where takeaway comes in. Don't feel guilty about it. Everyone's doing it. As long as you're not doing it every night, you've got nothing to worry about. Besides, some takeaway can be quite healthy and nowhere near as burnt as the food I cook.

When it comes to takeaway joints, loyalty is really important. If the food's good and you get looked after, you won't try anywhere else. If the guy from one takeaway place ever saw me buying from another one, I don't know if I could live with myself. That's just me.

We don't have takeaway too often, unless Nicky and the kids are away, in which case I usually don't start thinking about dinner until around 7.30 pm. By then it's too late to go and buy food and cook it. As a result I've tried heaps of different types of takeaway. Over the years I've developed a special liking for some more than others. After much thought and contemplation, I've managed to rate my top ten takeaway foods.

BILLY'S TOP TEN TAKEAWAY

10. The pie

You can't beat a good pie. I love the mystery you get with a pie. What's actually in it? How hot is it going to be? And when will it start repeating on me? There are lots of different varieties of pie now – I love a chicken pie and a bit of curry pie. Yum yum! Whatever is in it, it's very rare to find a pie at just the right eating temperature. It's either so cold that it's nearly a pie ice-cream or it's so hot that it burns your tongue, lips and the roof of your mouth to the point where you can't taste anything for a week. Four'N Twenties have separated us into two groups. Those people who stick the nozzle of the sauce bottle into the pastry and those who just put the sauce on top of the pastry. Personally, I like it on top. For those of you who are health freaks, just add a Kraft Single and a piece of beetroot to the top of your pie and hey-presto – instant salad pie.

Australian history time. We did not invent the meat pie. Sad but true. The Ancient Greeks got there first, then the French and English had a fair influence on its development. Early settlers bought the pie to us, we got organised with pie warmers and those boys walking through the crowds at the footy wearing pie boxes. Our claim to fame is that we made it our unofficial national dish. Australians eat over 500 000 000 pies each year. At finals time at the MCG, fans can consume 90 000 pies in a day.

9. The hotdog

I reckon this is easily the dodgiest of all takeaways. You'll never, ever deliberately go out to get a hotdog. But they somehow manage to find you. And they always do the job. Whether you're at the footy or you've just stumbled out of a nightclub, the humble hotdog will satisfy any tummy rumbling. There's also the added excitement of trying to pick which condiment you're going to have with it. You can choose from tomato sauce, mustard, cheese, chilli sauce, sauerkraut, coleslaw, pickle, relish, onion, lettuce and tomato. As Billy says, 'All of the above, please!' There was a hotdog joint in Geelong called Doggie Style and it was very popular. Heaps of people used to turn up but for all the wrong reasons.

Bread + some sort of sausage and some sort of sauce = winner. You don't need to be a brain to work that one out. I would have thought when blokes were inventing beer that they would have killed two birds with the one stone and invented a type of food that could be eaten with one hand. Some people claim the hotdog can be traced right back to the 1480s in Vienna, and others to the 17th century Germany. But the most important thing is that hotdogs, wherever they came from, were first sold at the baseball in America in 1893 by a German bloke. He owned an amusement park, a beer garden and a brewery and he decided to value add – sounds like a good bloke if you ask me! Why are they called 'hotdogs'? Sausages have been called 'dogs' since at least 1884 – something to do with dogmeat that I don't want to think about.

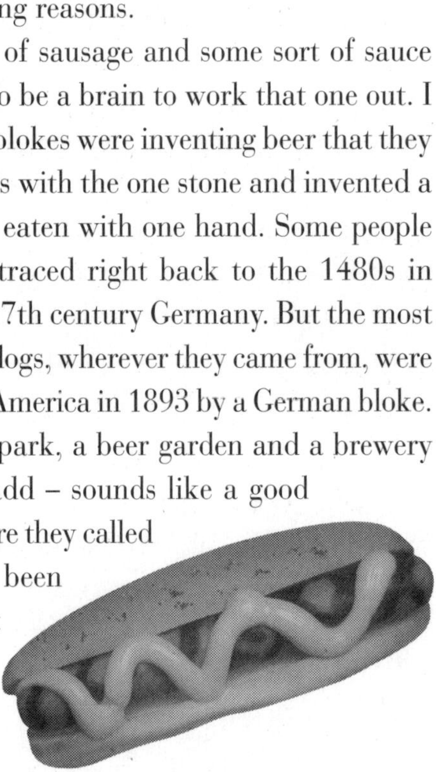

8. The souvlaki

This delicacy is only valid for consumption between the hours of 2 am and 5 am. My opinion on the souvlaki could be slightly clouded because I've never had one of these sober. Lamb or chicken? Chicken or lamb? A tough decision to make when you're half-tanked. Only get garlic sauce if you're going home alone. If you have garlic sauce and you're in the company of a female, she will not be able to get within 5 metres of you, even if she wants to. You know you've had a big night when you wake up with half a souvlaki lying in the bed next to you.

More Australian history: Melbourne has the third-largest Greek population in the world. In fact, 47 per cent of Australia's Greek population lives in Melbourne. The first large groups of Greek immigrants pulled into Port Phillip Bay in 1947 and I reckon they had seen a great business opportunity. They saw an untapped market in hungry drunk blokes roaming around late at night. The big questions are: if you're sober, does a souvlaki still fall apart? And does the garlic sauce still drip all over your clothes?

7. Indian

I'm not a massive fan of Indian cooking. I'd much rather watch them play cricket. I'll still have Indian occasionally. I like the way they do their meat, especially that butter chicken. But most of all, I like their roti bread. Sometimes, I'll even ask for a main course serving of it. One day I want to try mixing cultures by having vegemite on my roti bread.

?

Can fat people go skinny dipping?

6. Thai

I know this would appear much higher on a lot of people's lists but I haven't quite caught on yet. Don't get me wrong, it has its moments but I'm just not big on the really hot stuff. With me, it burns on the way in and burns on the way out. Heaps of my mates swear by it, though. They'd have it in their top three, if not number one. I haven't given up and am willing to keep at it to see if it can turn me around. It's always reasonably priced and the Thai people who work there are so polite and friendly. I plan on testing out their friendliness one night by doing a runner.

I reckon food has played a huge role in Australian history. At the same as a good bloke called Tom Wills got Australian Rules footy up and running 150 years ago, a couple of other blokes – Burke and a different Wills – set out to travel from the bottom of Australia to the top, taking two year's worth of food with them. They didn't do their sums properly, and some of the food went off, so that all except one person eventually died of starvation. A very important legacy of the Burke and Wills expedition is that everyone realised that horses and camels were not going to get us far, so we got into cars, and then servos sprang up everywhere. Anyway, some bright spark grabbed the business opportunity and country servos started selling food for travelers as well as petrol. Then eventually, city people cottoned on to the idea that other people were lazy and that's the short version of how takeaway food took off in Australia.

5. KFC/Macca's

When it comes to KFC, you can forget about all these new-fangled things like Popcorn Chicken and Zinger Burgers – give me Original Chicken anytime. And the best thing about KFC is you can get a whole bucket's worth of chicken. A bucket! Other places spend time worrying about upsizing their meals but how can you upsize a bucket? 'Would you like to upsize that bucket to a wheelie bin full of chicken?' The other good thing about KFC is those moist towelettes they give you. They actually clean the grease off your hands really well. They also clean the car really well.

I usually go to Macca's for a chocolate sundae. Every now and again I'll grab a Quarter Pounder and fries. But what I love about Macca's is that it's open virtually all the time. Some are open 24 hours. It's more about knowing that it's there. Even if I don't go, I can sleep easy at night knowing that if I get hungry, I can just go whenever I want.

4. Subway

The kids got me into Subway. It's supposed to be healthier. So I gave it a shot and liked what I had. In their TV ads they used that American bloke who lost a lot of weight by eating Subway. Simple campaign, but it worked. There are Subways popping up everywhere now. I know coz I keep stopping at them. If it's healthier, then it's OK if I eat twice as much.

Why do people put those 'baby on board' signs in their car? Do they think we are planning on hitting them?

3. Pizza

If every other food in the world disappeared then I have no doubt that I could live on pizza forever. Everyone has their favourite pizza. Some of us like variations on pizzas that are up on the board. Over time, I've developed my own pizza. It's chicken with BBQ sauce and semi-dried tomato. My pizza guy has got it down pat now. The great thing about pizza is that it's a very social takeaway meal. It's easy to share. It's cut into slices and everyone gets a feel for how much they should have or can get away with having. I don't like them when they're delivered. That pizza warming bag thingo makes them go a bit soggy.

The world's first pizza shop, Lombardi's, started as a grocery store in New York in 1897 and the family kept it going until 1984. The idea in the beginning was that you'd buy a slice, whatever size you could afford, of a kind of tomato pie. We didn't cotton on until 1961 when Toto's Pizza House opened in Melbourne in Lygon Street, Carlton. What did blokes have for breakfast after a big night before cold pizza was invented?

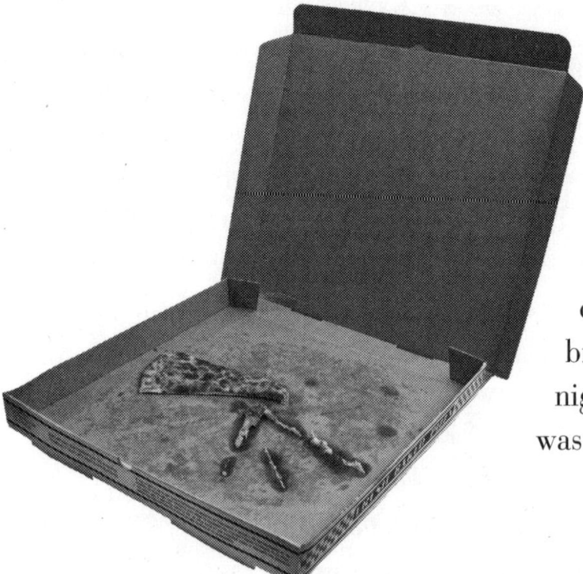

2. Fish and chips

Fish and chips – how good! Mmmm, so many different things, all fried in oil. It's amazing how good things taste when they're deep-fried. Someone once tried doing it with a Mars Bar and wouldn't you know it – a big hit! When I get fish and chips, I usually just go for the standards – a piece of flake, chips, a potato cake and a couple of dimmies. There's so much else up on the fish and chip board that I haven't tried or seen people try. Which makes me wonder what they're still doing up there. Does anyone eat cornjacks? What about crab sticks and banana and pineapple fritters? Why have other fish up on the board? Who's going to the fish and chip shop to have blue eye, flounder, hake (what is that?), couta or whiting?

My favourite thing to do with fish and chips is to keep them in their wrapper and rip a hole in the top. They stay hotter a lot longer. Those first couple of times you stick your hand in to grab some chips is a real test of your will because it's just so bloody hot in there. You have to be careful not to let your chips stay in there too long, though, otherwise they get soggy. I know there are some soggy chip fans out there but I prefer them crisp. That's just the way it is. I like my chips crisp and my family like their chips crisp and we make no apologies for that. When you've finished, don't throw out the wrapper. You'll miss out on the big bonus of unrolling the paper and discovering a couple of stray chips who tried to make a run for it.

?

If we throw rice at weddings,
do the Chinese throw pies?

I've noticed a trend. Lots of takeaway Chinese food now comes in these paper boxes with chopsticks. Us blokes like the old clear plastic containers because they come in handy in the shed. I keep all my screws in one, nails in another and so on. And think about the waste of these paper ones – you can't reuse them. So, this is a plea to think about the environment: all you blokes out there, start asking for the plastic containers which will ensure the supply keeps up. Just don't let the Darl throw them out because that would be wasteful. I've actually got a whole section in my shed for my empty plastic container collection.

1. Chinese

After much arguing in my own head, I finally decided that Chinese takeaway is my number one. It's been around the longest of the Asian takeaways and has taken a battering (sorry!) from the new kids on the block like Thai and Indian, but it's toughed it out and survived. I really admire that. Once you find good Chinese you are set and you will be their loyal customer until they move or sell the business to a dodgy relative or the premises mysteriously burns down. If you're feeling like something simple, you can grab a fried rice. Can't go wrong with a fried rice. If you want something a bit more substantial, then there are heaps of options.

I love it when a new Chinese restaurant opens and the word gets around that the chef has come from a well-known Chinese restaurant like the Flower Drum. Only to find out later that it's the Flower Drum in Yarrawonga.

So, there you have it. Chinese comes out on top. Mmmm ... this chapter's made me really hungry. I may have to stop at Subway on the way and then KFC – the chicken comes in a bucket! A bucket! Have I mentioned that?

Riverina schoolboys back in grade 5. I'm the good looking blond on the end.

Mateship

Macca, Herbie, Bluey and Simmo. Somewhere out there, these blokes are someone's mates. We all have them. Many of them go back to primary school days or grew up on the same street or played footy together. Somehow, without any official ceremony, they became mates, attached forever. Mateship is entrenched in this country's history. Our boys fighting together at Gallipoli and enduring the hardships at Changi prisoner of war camp personify the concept of mateship. They maintained a special bond of support and friendship and would cheer each other up using humour. This is what modern mateship is based upon. Mates are there for each other at all times. They also keep you grounded. If your head starts getting too big, your mates are the first ones to pull you down a few pegs.

Mates can fall into different categories. There are good mates, close mates, work mates, old mates and there are even ones that are 'a mate of a mate'. Once you become a mate, you have to take on the role of a mate. You need to have an understanding and commitment between each other. There are generally accepted rules that mates must abide by which have developed over time and been passed down through generations of blokes. They have never been written down – until now.

BILLY'S RULES FOR MATES

- Know the order of a shout. When it's your turn to shout, just jump up and get 'em. Don't wait to be asked (please take note Gav and Johnno). Being in the toilet when it's your shout is heavily frowned upon.

- You must keep up in a shout. Be ready for the next beer when it arrives. Don't fall behind and try to opt out, no matter what the excuse. It looks like you've either gone soft or are just being a tight arse.

- A true mate teaches himself to carry a minimum of four beers at a time through a crowded bar. Upon seeing this, another mate is permitted to undo the drink carrier's pants so that they fall to the floor. The drink carrier is to continue on his journey and deliver the beers without spilling a drop.

- Never go and see a movie together. That's what couples do. Blokes don't watch movies together. Unless it's at a buck's night.

- Never, ever, sleep with a mate's girlfriend, even after they've split up. Some mates have a ten year cap on this; if ten years has passed since the split, then the rule expires.

- You must at some stage, as a group of mates, play in an indoor cricket team together. Your team must have a stupid name that involves a play on words, a bad pun or a double entendre (e.g. The Ball Tamperers).

- Don't hesitate to lend a mate money if he needs it. You'll get it back eventually, after it has made its way through his TAB phone account.

- Be a good wingman. If you're out and a mate looks like picking up, you have to keep the girl's friend entertained, even if it means having to dance with her. You will not sway from your duty in wooing this girl even if you find her unattractive. We've all taken a hit for our mates over the years.

- Never dance with a mate. It's not a good look and you're wasting your time. Girls never come up to two guys who are dancing and start dancing with them.

- If a mate is moving house, you must help. Simple.

- Never get one of your mates to be a godparent for your child. They make the worst godparents ever. They never remember their godchild's birthday. Relatives make much better godparents.

- Whenever you get together, no mate is immune from having shit hung on him. Everyone there is expected to play an active part in bagging the crap out of each other for the majority of the time you're together.

?

Why does a bloke who wants to punch you say 'What's your problem?' when he has no intention of solving it for you?

- Always be prepared to play a game of cricket or 'kick to kick' without notice.

- If you are both drunk and tired, you may share a bed with a mate but you must be fully clothed at all times and never mention to anybody that it ever happened.

- If a mate gets into a fight you must fly the flag and help him out. If you're outnumbered, be prepared to get your head kicked in. Having said that, there is no shame in walking away (well, most likely running away). If it looks way too dangerous, everyone get the hell out of there.

- If a mate comes around for a drink, never offer him a cheaper beer than the ones he's brought with him. It looks like you're keeping his good beers while getting rid of your crap ones.

- If you go to a mate's place for a drink always take half a dozen stubbies (they must be still in their packaging).

- As a group of mates, work out where you stand on the issue of light beer. Personally, I think it's easier just to ban it from every function. If a designated driver insists on having light beer, then it must be kept in a separate room to the full-strength beer, so that there is no chance of them getting mixed up.

- Never be caught by another mate drinking a Bacardi Breezer or a Vodka Cruiser. Not even for a one in between or a change up. Your sexuality will be questioned and it could result in you having your mateship suspended.

- Form a gambling syndicate with your mates or, at the very least, go in a regular Quaddie together. Any big win must be spent on a boozy golf weekend away.

- If you're a qualified tradesman or even an unqualified but self-taught one, then you must help a mate with a job around his house that falls under your area of expertise. The only payment you can accept is a slab of beer.

- Without doubt, the most important rule for mates is 'The Code of Silence' or 'The Vault' or, as it is more commonly known, 'What happens on the footy trip, stays on the footy trip'.

Hopefully, you never get to the point where you need to remind a mate about one or more of these rules. If that's the case then you will seriously have to consider his future as a mate. If need be, convene a special meeting of mates and give him the opportunity to explain himself to the group. After considering his plea for mercy, have a vote on whether or not he is worthy of being a mate anymore. If he can no longer cut it, then you have no choice but to revoke his mateship and let him go and join that ever growing new group of men who have lost their way – metrosexuals.

Some drinking games

As people have probably already worked out, I love a beer and I've been known to have a few on a hot day. But when it comes to having a beer, I'd much rather be surrounded by my mates than sitting at home by myself. Me and my mates often go down to the TAB, get into a shout, put 25 bucks each into a kitty and then take it in turns having a bet on the horses. I must admit I do like to have a punt on the dogs as well. The race is over in 30 seconds, the winning numbers come up quick and there's never a protest coz there's no jockeys to influence the result. This is close to being my perfect day. I'm not religious but I'd be happy if that's what heaven was like. A little Billy tip: when in doubt, back the red dog (number 1).

If you are at someone's house and having a few frothies (my beer of choice: VB), you can always add another element to the drinking by playing some drinking games. They're always good value and help you get pissed quicker. Before people write in to complain, I just want to say that I am all for the responsible consumption of alcohol. Always know who and where your designated driver is. It's pretty simple. He'll be the one sitting in the corner, looking bored and having a shit time.

?

If you choke a smurf what colour will it turn?

So, what I've done with this chapter is try to think of good drinking games that I've played, that are pretty simple and don't require too much stuff. Have a read and give some of 'em a go. You're sure to have fun … and probably get hammered. Before you read on, I would just like to say that I will not be held responsible for any stupid behaviour and/or public nudity that result from the playing of these games.

BOTTLES (also known as 'Sevens')

Number of players: 4–10

Equipment required: none

Billy's rating: 8/10

How to play

This game is a lot of fun but requires a bit of concentration (not one of my strong points). You need a few players for this one. At least four is a good start. Everyone sits in a circle and one person starts counting with '1'. The person on their left continues the count by saying '2' and the next person says '3' and so on. When someone gets to a number that has something to do with the number 7 they must say the word 'bottles' in place of the number. It could be a number with a 7 in it, like 17, or a number that is a multiple of 7, like 21. If someone stuffs up, they have to skol their drink. The game then starts again. Remember when you were a kid at school and you'd say, 'Maths, what a waste of time! When am I ever going to need to use the times tables in the future?' Now here's an answer: for playing drinking games.

WOMBAT

Number of players: minimum of 2
Equipment required: none
Billy's rating: 9/10

How to play

This game's called Wombat for no particular reason. It's just a funny sounding animal. I've found that this game suits your smaller party. It works like this: Everyone sits around drinking beers. The catch is – you have to hold your drink with your non-preferred hand, i.e. if you're right handed, hold it with your left. If anyone catches you drinking out of your good hand, they yell out 'Wombat!' and you have to skol your drink. Doesn't sound like much but as the night goes on, it really kicks in. People start forgetting which hand they're drinking out of and get themselves into all sorts of trouble. A difficult game for me to play because I've usually got drinks in both hands.

Here's a thought: maybe this game is called wombat because some species of them are endangered, just like blokes. A good example is the Southern Hairy-nosed Wombat (*Lasiorhinus latifrons*) which looks a bit like this one (who looks like he's downed a few frothies). Apparently there are circumstances and factors threatening its survival. Keep up the battle, little fella – us hairy-nosed species need to stick together.

ONE SMART FELLOW

Number of players: minimum of 4
Equipment required: none
Billy's rating: 8/10

How to play

This game combines alcohol with the tongue twister. A diabolical mix. Everyone sits in a circle and someone starts off by saying: 'One smart fellow, he felt smart.' The person to their left continues by saying: 'Two smart fellows, they felt smart.' The next person says: 'Three smart fellows, they felt smart' … and so on. You need to keep the speed up, to put pressure on the next person. It doesn't take much to work out what people say when they stuff it up. When they do, they have to skol their drink and the game starts again. The longer you play and the more people drink, the harder this game gets. Usually, when it gets around to me, to save time I just start skolling my drink.

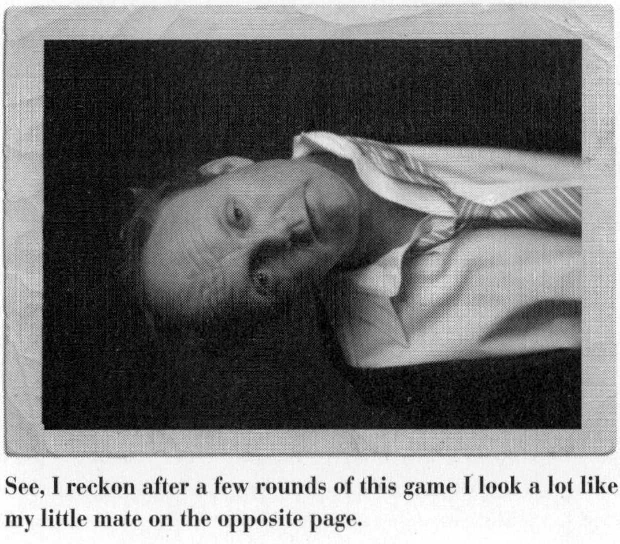

See, I reckon after a few rounds of this game I look a lot like my little mate on the opposite page.

BOTTLE TOPS

Number of players: minimum of 2
Equipment required: one bottle top per player
Billy's rating: 7/10

How to play

This drinking game is a game of skill. So it's right up my alley. You have to sit opposite your opponent but not too close. You'll be able to judge the distance based on the surface you're using. You each have a glass of beer in front of you. You then have to bounce the bottle top off the surface (the ground or a table) and into the other person's drink. If you get it in their drink, they have to skol it. To avoid anyone choking, make sure the bottle top is taken out of the drink before it is skolled.

Another thing in danger of extinction: the bottle opener. It's under threat from twist tops. There's an upside though – because there was never one around when you needed it most (at 2 am), the fact that you can open a stubby without one has led to great savings in dental care and fewer eye-socket accidents.

WATER TANKED

Number of players: minimum of 4
Equipment required: big bowl or vase, cup, bottle of water
Billy's rating: 8/10

How to play

This game requires a bit of preparation, so if you can't be stuffed or are already too drunk to care, move on to the next game. If you're still with us, then go and get a big bowl or vase and fill it with water. You then have to place a cup in the vase and fill the cup about halfway with water. You'll also need another bottle filled with water. Each person must pour some water from that bottle into the cup. The person who makes the cup sink has to skol their drink. You just set it up again and the person who skolled last starts it off again. The more you drink the harder it is to control how much water you're pouring in. This game may be banned if we reach Stage 5 water restrictions.

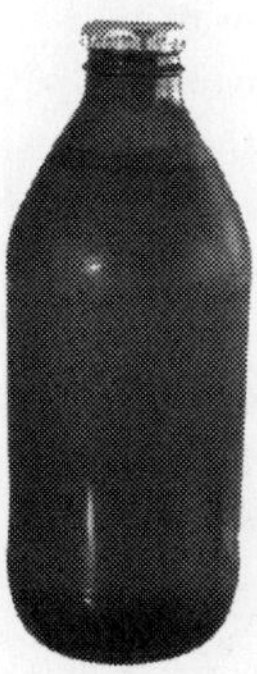

As a beer drinker, I'm proud to continue an ancient tradition – brewing (and therefore, drinking) is one of the oldest forms of manufacturing known to man. So blokes have had their priorities right from the word go! A bloke called John Boston brewed Australia's first beer in 1794 in Sydney. Then a smart fellow called John Moss set up Melbourne's first brewery in 1838 behind a pub in Flinders Street. Then Fosters Brewing Company thought the punters would like a cold beer in summer and started producing Foster's Lager in 1888. It was an instant hit and the rest is history.

BOAT RACES

Number of players: 2 teams of at least 4 players
Equipment required: none
Billy's rating: 8/10

How to play

This is an old favourite. You have two teams of four (or more) standing in single file. The opposition team faces towards you. Each person has a pot of beer (preferably a large one). Someone says 'ready, set, go', and the person at the front of each team has to skol their drink. When they're finished they have to turn the glass upside down on their head and then the next person in line skols and so on. It's just like a relay to the end. I've seen a version of this game played where the last person in the line (the anchor) has to skol two beers. If you have a number of knockout rounds, then the winning teams could be pretty tanked come the final.

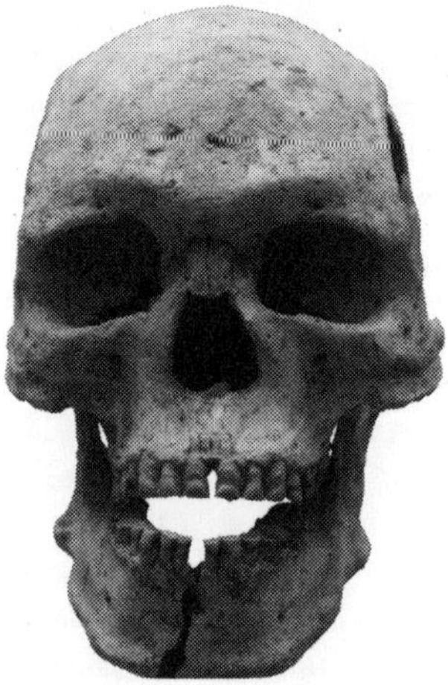

~~skol~~ ~~scull~~ skull

Isn't the English language confusing? No wonder I could never pass the spelling tests at school. 'Skol' means 'to consume a drink at one draught'. Draught! Sounds the same as 'draft' (as in 'picks') but looks way more complicated. Then there's 'scull' which is a rowing term. And 'skull', as in your head without the fleshy bits. In fact, I'm having trouble getting this all through my thick skull, but I think this drinking game is called 'boat races' because you skol drinks while you're in a team, like a rowing scull. Better get myself another frothie after all that thinking!

GARY ABLETT JNR

Number of players: minimum of 3
Equipment required: TV
Billy's rating: 9/10

How to play

Gather round the telly with your mates and watch a Geelong game. Every time you see Gary Ablett Jnr cop a kidney punch from his tagger, skol a beer. Guaranteed you'll be pissed by half-time.

BILLY'S ULTIMATE DRINKING GAME

Number of players: minimum of 1
Equipment required: none
Billy's rating: 10/10

How to play

Step 1: Fill your glass with VB.
Step 2: Empty glass into mouth.
Step 3: Swallow.
Repeat steps 1–3 until you reach the desired effect.

Even more wisdom from Blighty

One of the least pleasant experiences as a footballer is to get a blast from the coach. Whether it be an individual or team ear bashing, it's not much fun sitting there and copping an angry outburst. Every coach has at least a couple a year and they almost always follow a pretty piss-poor effort on the team's part. Blighty was no different. He'd get angry every now and again but in typical Blighty fashion, he'd always give it his own special touch.

It's 1992 and we're playing Adelaide at Football Park. We've got a terrible record here. Haven't even got close to winning a game. None of us were looking forward to coming over. Not a great attitude to be going into the game with. True to form, the first half is a disaster. We make a sluggish start, which you can't afford to do here, and before too long we're getting smashed all around the ground. I'm not getting much of a touch but I'm not alone. We haven't got one winner out there. This is going to be a long day. The siren goes for half-time and we're down by eleven goals. We trudge off the ground with our heads bowed and go into the rooms.

There's an eerie, hushed mood in the rooms. Before we've had time to sit down, Blighty wanders in and summons us all into the little rev up room. I'm thinking, you never know with Blighty. You might think he's going to go one way with something and then he goes the other. Maybe he won't be angry with us. Maybe he'll take the opposite approach and start reading from a joke book. As trainers begin approaching players with ice, we get a sense of where Blighty's head is at. He quickly roars in a loud, stern voice: 'No bloody ice, no bloody drinks, just straight into the room!'

We all slowly shuffle into the room. You're never in a hurry to cop a major pasting. Hopefully, the longer it takes us to get in there, the more time Blighty has to settle down a little bit. Us more-experienced players head straight for the back of the room, out of reach. When I say that, I mean that we were *just* out of reach. These rooms are tiny, with barely enough room to fit the 22 players, the coach and a whiteboard. All the players are now in and we're just waiting on Blighty. The longer we wait, the more we're crapping our dacks.

Blighty storms in and slams the door behind him so hard that it's barely hanging from its hinges. He then wastes no time in giving us an almighty spray, which Malcolm is very good at. Our eyes are completely focussed on him as he strides back and forth across the room, his bellowing voice vibrating every bone in our bodies. This is the angriest and loudest outburst I've ever heard from a coach. All of a sudden, he stops yelling, walks over to the light switch and turns it off. Now we're all

Who closes the door when the bus driver gets off?

sitting in the dark. It's pitch black. I don't know if any of you people out there have ever been squashed into a tiny room with twenty other blokes and a raving madman but I can tell you, it's a not a good place to be. It's silent but you know he's in there somewhere. You're just waiting for his next explosion. Not being able to see him, you won't know where it'll come from. Then, without warning, comes this enormous, booming voice that makes me and everyone else jump a mile in the air. I'm desperately trying to listen to where he is moving to in the room but I can't follow him. He yells again from another part of the room and we all jump out of our skins again. He then moves to somewhere else in the room and yells again. I'm looking here, there and everywhere. My heart's pumping. I'm sweating. I don't know if I'm Arthur or Martha!

The next thing you know, he bangs the whiteboard so hard with his fist that it causes his watch to fly off. We hear it smash and then land in pieces across the room. It would be hilarious under any other circumstances but it just scares us into thinking, great, he's going to be even angrier now. There's a bit more silence. Then the lights come back on. The six blokes in the front row are sitting there with their heads in their hands as if they thought they were going to get belted. Malcolm gives us one last stare and then calmly walks out of the room.

Nobody can move. Blighty mightn't be in the room anymore but the steam that came out of his ears is still hovering about. That was some blast. My ears are still ringing. A couple of the boys look like they need to call their mums. I suppose there's nothing left for us to do but get back out there and really put in for the second half. Eleven goals is gettable if you break it down into six goals a quarter. If ever we were going to pull off a miracle, it's going to be today. We've just had the biggest foot put up our arses. This could turn out to be one of the greatest comebacks in Geelong's history.

We run back out onto ground for the start of the third quarter. Everything looks different and smells different. It's as if we've detoxed at half-time. I feel like I've been cleansed. We take control early and kick a couple of goals. The momentum's in our favour. They get the next couple and pretty much close the game out and shatter our renewed confidence with a quarter and a half to play. We get rolled big time. Not my best game, either. It is the slowest I've ever walked off the ground, especially at Football Park. But I'd rather stay out here and take the abuse from the Adelaide crowd than risk going back into the rooms to face Blighty.

I eventually walk up the race and into the rooms. I'm going to have to face the music sooner or later. To my surprise the atmosphere in the rooms is pretty relaxed. Blighty's just wandering around and chatting to blokes. After a while, he goes to the corner of the room, sits by himself and reflects on what has been a pretty draining day. It gives me an idea. I go back into the little rev up room and start gathering up all the pieces of Blighty's broken watch. I'm going to get this fixed, I think to myself. He'll be blown away. It'll be a great moment between me and my coach.

Those bits of broken watch are still in the bottom of my bag. It's up in the cupboard.

The birds and the bees talk

Ah yes, the dreaded birds and the bees talk. More often than not, it's the mothers who give the talk. Fathers tend to shirk it. It's as if they're trying to pick up a footy with Matthew Scarlett bearing down on them. They don't want to know about it. But as a dad, you need to play an active part in educating your kids about all things in life, including sex. Sure, it's an awkward topic to talk about. My father's chat to me went something like this. I'm in the lounge room watching telly. Dad walks in and says, 'Billy, you got any questions?' I look up with a confused expression on my face and go, 'Questions? About what? Nah, I haven't got any questions.' Dad says, 'Fine,' and walks out of the room and straight to Mum, boasting about how he's just given me the talk. Thanks for nothin', Dad. I was that kid at school who always laughed at the dirty jokes and then had to ask another mate to explain them to me later. I had no idea. Up until I was about ten years old, I thought circumcised kids looked that way coz their dads were bald.

Fortunately for me, my parents ran a newsagency, so I did manage to learn something from reading *Playboy* magazine. When I say reading, I mean looking. When I say looking, I mean perving. September was full of nightmares for me when it came to footy but give me Miss September anytime. It did, however, give me the wrong impression of women. I thought that whenever a woman was naked she'd have the urge to get down on all fours, squeeze her boobs between her arms and have a seductive look on her face. Which I quickly learnt wasn't the case, when I accidentally walked in on Nanna getting out of the bath.

Your kids need to know about sex. The more knowledge they have, the better equipped they'll be to deal with it. So, have that chat with them. Don't be one of those parents who keeps putting it off because you're embarrassed. It'll be a lot more embarrassing trying to talk to them about it when they're 25 years old. Having said that, don't force the issue.

A good place to start is to find out about what they're being taught at school. That'll let you know how much they've already learnt. Most schools have a pretty good program. A lot better than when I was at school. It was an all boys school and the only sex ed the boys got was when I remembered to bring my *Playboy* magazines to school. Which reminds me, Shanno, I'm still waiting for you to give me one back.

One of the best ways to ease into a discussion at home is to buy a book about sex, give it to your kids and say to them, have a read of this and then come and ask me any questions

?

Why can't women put on mascara with their mouth closed?

Peach-faced Lovebirds
(***agapornis roseicollis***)]

Ever wondered where 'the birds and the bees' expression came from? Well, apparently we're meant to look at nature and learn a thing or two. It comes from way back when the poet Samuel Coleridge wrote: 'All nature seems at work ... The bees are stirring – birds are on the wing ... and I the while, the sole unbusy thing, not honey make, nor pair, nor build, nor sing.' I don't really get poetry to tell the truth. Maybe it means I should try a new line on the Darl: 'Do you want make honey tonight?'

you've got. Or you can be really thorough and tell them to summarise each chapter because there'll be a test on it next week. There are some good books out there which, in the end, can do half the work for you. It's just a matter of actually getting your kids to read it. Maybe one of the kids' favourite book series could come to the party and combine their popular character with some sex ed as well. I'll have a word to Garry Lyon about doing a new book called 'Specky Magee and the Rude Bits'.

There are ways to make your kids feel more comfortable discussing the topic of sex at home. One is to not make a big deal of it when you find out that they have their first boyfriend or girlfriend. Make it sound like a very natural, normal thing for them to be doing. Don't get too excited. Don't stir them up by saying things like, 'Ooooh, lovers!' and don't ask a lot of prying questions. Be supportive and let them know that you're always available if they need to chat about anything, even if you're watching the footy (except for the grand final, of course, which should never be interrupted unless it's an emergency, in which case they should try 000 first).

When it comes to discussing the nitty-gritty of lovemaking, some people find it easier to use an analogy instead of explaining the actual details. Personally, I reckon just go with the real stuff. The analogies just end up sounding a bit weird. But if you want to use one, I've come up with one for you: 'Imagine a woman is like an airport and a man is like a plane which is coming in to land. All of the plane's little passengers

?

Are there male ladybirds?

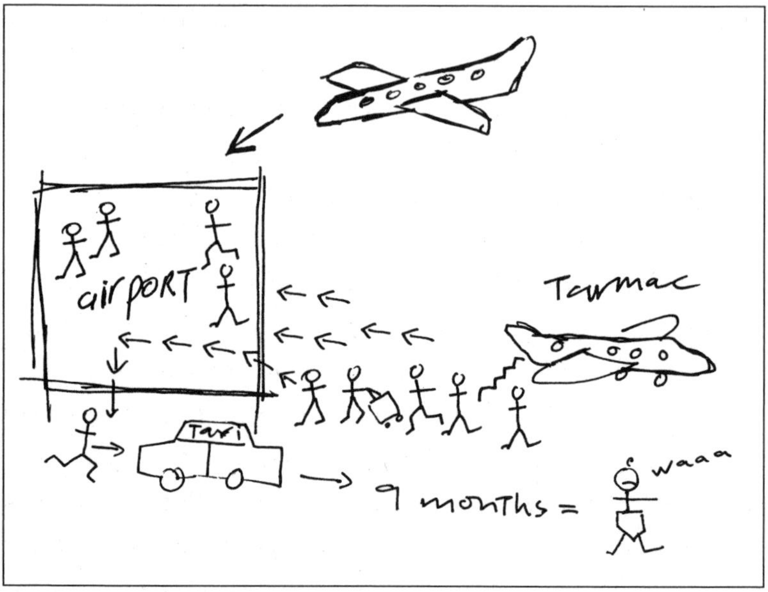

Blighty-esque in its simplicity.

get off and go through the terminal. After they make their way through the airport they notice that there is only one taxi waiting at the taxi rank. If one of the passengers makes it to that taxi and gets in, then in nine months' time there'll be a baby.' Yeah, I think I nailed that. It was easier than I thought. Millions of parents around the country will be thanking me for that one. It is important to add that sometimes the airport can be closed due to a baggage or domestic dispute. Whatever you do, do not redirect the flight to another airport. Keep circling until you get the go-ahead to land. Please note: Don't disappoint the airport by having the passengers disembark too quickly.

Be open about contraception. Have some around the house. If that's a bit too full-on for you, then place them carefully where they can be found. 'Hey, look what just came out of the cornflakes packet.' Or 'Look what the Easter Bunny left this year.' You can always make an appointment for your kids with a doctor, who will go through the suitable forms of contraception with them. Teaching your teenage kids about safe sex could be the most important thing you do for them.

Don't let your child's gender decide what or how much you tell them. Whether they're a boy or a girl, they should get all the necessary information. When it comes to sex, fathers, over the years, have been a lot stricter on their daughters than on their sons. Some fathers would be happy if their daughters were locked in their rooms until they were 35. When it came to their sons, on the other hand, they'd say to them, 'I've got three words of advice – go for it! I mean it. Here are some condoms, knock yourself out. I'll be handing out trophies at the end of the year; let's see who gets three votes this week.' Sons and daughters should be given equal time.

You need to remember that times have changed. Don't even think about starting a discussion on sex with the phrase 'back in my day'. Back in your day they didn't have text messaging or access to sex on the internet. So, know your stuff. There you go, I've just given you a legitimate research reason for looking up porn on the net.

Alright, there you have it. I've given you the information and the inspiration to go out there and talk to your teenagers about sex. At the very least, you can feel good about getting it over and done with. If you still think you need more help, then I'll check under my bed. I'm sure I've still got some copies of *Playboy* I can lend you. If all else fails – go and ask your mother.

The Brownless Olympics

The Olympic Games are the ultimate when it comes to sport. If you win the men's 100 metres then you're the fastest man in the world. That's the whole world. Out of the six-and-a-half billion people on this earth – you are the quickest. That's right, even faster that David Wojcinski. That's quite an achievement when you think about it. For your efforts you get a gold medal, the adoration of your countrymen, a couple of cheap looking commercials for a deodorant company and a question mark forever hanging over your head about whether you were on steroids.

Not all of us can make it to the lofty heights of such an elite international competition but that doesn't stop us dreaming about it. Every time an Australian wins gold and they play the national anthem, I imagine that's me up there. Some Olympic moments are stuck in our heads forever. I'll never forget the tuna fisherman from Port Lincoln, Dean Lukin, with his arms wobbling as he lifted that bar above his head to win gold in the weightlifting. There's something about the Olympics that really gets the adrenalin and the emotion flowing. We follow the trials and tribulations of our athletes so closely that when it comes to them performing, we are virtually out there running alongside them. Anyone who witnessed Cathy Freeman's win in the 400 at the Sydney Olympics says that it was the most amazing experience of their life. There wasn't a dry eye in the stadium. Me and my brothers were no different from every other Aussie. We knew we'd never represent our country and compete against the best in the world but that didn't stop us devising our version of the Olympics in our very own backyard. We'd use whatever we could find that was lying around and somehow managed to include heaps of events in our unique Brownless Olympics. Sure, most of the equipment didn't conform to international standards but we didn't care. We still kept our own records, many of which I hold and which still stand today.

Javelin

Simple. A cricket stump. Sure, a bit shorter than a normal javelin (by about 2 metres) but that was all we had. And you could throw it a mile. We had pretty good stumps. They had metal tips, so they would stick into the ground like a javelin, or into my brother's foot, if he wasn't paying attention. The problem was that the stump was a bit more difficult to grip than a normal javelin, especially after the time my brother sabotaged mine by oiling it down before the event. For his actions, he was brought before our Olympic committee and punished by being held down and having his arm punched repeatedly until he said sorry.

High jump

No backyard Olympics would be complete without the high jump. As a kid it's your favourite event. You get to jump over something and land on a mat. It used to feel great. This was the first piece of equipment we built. We had two sticks as the

BASIC EQUIPMENT LIST

Think about encouraging your kids to stage their own Backyard Olympics while the 2008 Olympics are on the telly. That way, you do your bit to prevent childhood obesity by encouraging them to be active, and you get to have the couch and the telly to yourself. By the way, have a good look at the takeaway chapter to get my top suggestions for sustenance during the two weeks of intense Olympic viewing.

Here's a quick reference for what you need:

Broomstick (cross bar for both high jump and hurdle)

Round rock (substitute shotput)

Bricks (to build hurdles – steal from neighbours if necessary)

Cricket stump (doubles nicely as javelin)

Shovel (to transport sand for long jump)

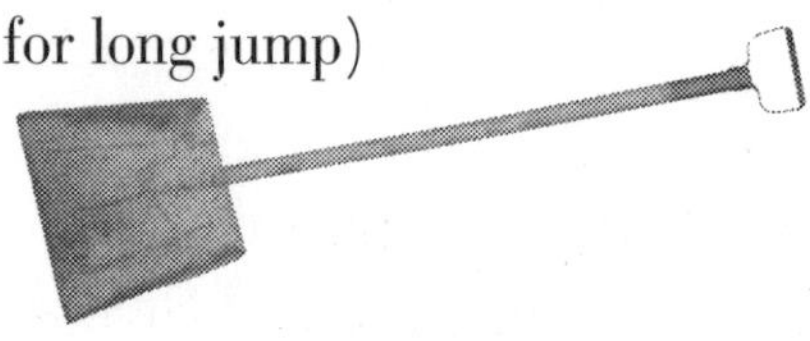

N.B. You can't tell the kids to drag a mattress outside for a landing pad for the high jump because the Olympic Committee (the Darl) would come down on you (and them) like a ton of bricks. But you need to remind them that they need something nice and soft to land on. This is encouraging them to think for themselves and to take responsibility for their actions.

upright poles, with nails in them for the different heights and a broomstick as the bar. For our landing mat we'd use a mattress that we'd take off one of our beds and drag out into the yard when Mum wasn't looking. Away we'd go, doing the 'Fosbury flop', which resulted in you landing on the mattress on your back. Unfortunately, it didn't have the same give as your proper high jump mat. In fact, it wasn't much better than landing on the ground. If you collected the broomstick bar on the way and landed on that as well, you were in a lot of trouble. It was the ultimate back breaker.

Hurdles

For the hurdles we would put sticks on some stacked bricks. Took a while to set up, pain in the arse really, but they worked a treat. If you hit one it wasn't anywhere near as painful as hitting proper hurdles. The stick would just fall off and your knee wouldn't cop much of a bang. There was the odd occasion when you'd knock the stick off and both of your legs would get entangled in the stick and you'd end up doing an almighty face plant. Very difficult to recover from and get back into the race. Pretty funny, though, if it wasn't you.

Long jump

We dug a hole in the ground and filled it up with sand. It just took us a while to get all of the sand. There's only so much you can take from the next door neighbour's sand pit before they start noticing. So, with each trip to the beach we'd bring a couple of bucket loads back with us to help top it up. It was the only long jump pit in the world that had sea shells and a couple of crabs in it.

100 Metres

Well, more like 50 metres. But it was long enough for us. We marked out the track on our block. How you went often depended on what lane you were in. Lane 3 had a dip in it about halfway up. If you didn't allow for it in your stride then you'd go arse over tit. Lane 4 had an ant hill in it that needed to be negotiated and lane 1 had those prickly bindies and was not to be run in with bare feet. We eventually found our sprint event being influenced by the Stawell Gift. We started handicapping ourselves and moved the finish line so that it was only about 2 feet from the fence.

Cycling

The yard wasn't big enough for the cycling, so we did it around the street. This added a minor obstacle in the form of cars backing out of their driveways. A seven-length lead could be easily cut back by the rider ploughing straight into a reversing Commodore and flying over the boot. The pressure and competition was very close to what you'd see in international cycling except that our dragsters weren't quite as aerodynamic. There were some classic finishes in the cycling. Unfortunately, the finishing line (usually someone's letterbox) wasn't equipped with a camera to record the photo finish.

?

Why do people say, 'you've been working like a dog' when dogs just sit around all day doing nothing?

Shot put

After a brief search we found a big, grey and fairly rounded rock that became our shot put. Its official weight was 'bloody heavy'. There wasn't a lot to the shot put, really. You'd hold it under your chin, sway back and forth a couple of times and then let her go with one almighty push and a loud grunt. Not a lot to it, that is, until yours truly spent a few hours watching the best shot putters in the world on telly. They would start crouched down at one end of the circle and then spin around twice before releasing the shot put with added momentum. I studied this method for a while and practised for a few weeks. It was then time to unleash my new technique on my brothers. They'd both already thrown and then I came up with my 'spin and throw' style and bam, I've launched this shot put into orbit. It's landed a good metre past theirs. They couldn't believe it. They were shell shocked. I dominated that event for consecutive Olympics.

The Brownless Olympics were fiercely competitive and no matter whether you were slightly injured or had the flu, you would always take part. The Olympic spirit was alive and well in the Brownless backyard. There mightn't have been a huge stadium but I could always hear the crowd screaming. In our minds it was as close to the real thing as you could get.

The day I punched on with Gazza

After the heartbreak of losing the '92 Grand Final it was time to harden up, so for the pre-season in '93, Malcolm Blight decided to introduce boxing into our training program. We'd go down to the gym, don all the proper head gear and gloves, hop into a ring and have these one on one sparring sessions. Malcolm thought it was good for your confidence. Well, let me tell you – if you can't fight, it's no good for your confidence. How it worked was you'd pretty much arrive and just pair up. The problem was that no-one ever wanted to spar with Gazza coz he used to be able to really go. And I mean really go. He'd grown up with six brothers and in that sort of environment you learn to look after yourself and more. We all knew the type of damage he was capable of doing and like everyone else, there was no way I was going to take him on.

It comes round to that time of the week again when we all have to rock up for the boxing session. I do the usual thing, where I wander in and start looking around for an easy opponent to pair up with (like Barry Stoneham or Sean Simpson), when, all of a sudden, there's Gazza standing right in front of me. He looks me in the eye and says, 'OK, Billy, you and me – let's have a spar.' So I say, 'No worries,' take my gear off and go and sit in the spa. He says, 'No, you idiot, get out here!'

After pacing around for a while and thinking about calling my loved ones, I eventually put the gloves and head guard on. I try to squeeze two head guards on for added protection but Blighty isn't having a bar of it. 'Just get out there, son!' There's no escaping it. The cards have been dealt. It's going to be me versus Gazza in the mismatch of the century. What it would boil down to is me being able to survive three 2-minute rounds of punishment from the great man. Our fitness coach, Phillip Walsh, has just bought this new-fandangled timer, which would go off every 2 minutes. He's pretty excited about it and so am I coz at the very least, I know that I won't have to spend a second longer than necessary in there getting pummelled.

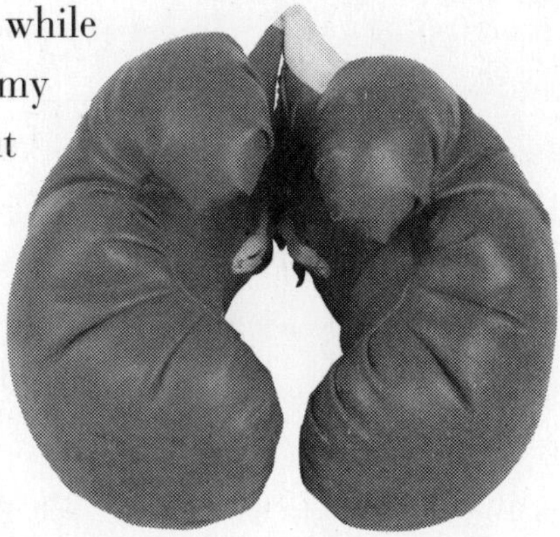

I enter the makeshift ring singing 'Eye of the Tiger' in my own head, in an effort to give myself some sense of false hope. Gazza jumps in like he's done it a million times before and then he starts marking his territory by bouncing around and practising some signature boxing moves. At this stage, the other boys are doing their weights but a few stop and gather around us. They can smell blood and can't wait to watch Gazza slaughter his next victim. The 'Eye of the Tiger' tune in my head suddenly turns into the Wiggles' 'Mash potato,

?

Why do big, tough boxers fight for a purse?

mash potato' or whatever it is. Before I know it, the bell goes and we're into round 1.

I somehow manage to keep Gazza at bay and scrape through the first round by staying out of his reach and covering up. The sound of the new timer, to end the round, is like music to my ears. I can't believe it. I've got through round 1 without having to take a dive. Round 2 begins and Gazza decides to be more adventurous. Being a big fan of Muhammad Ali, he starts mimicking his hero. He does the old Muhammad Ali 'hold one hand up in the air'. I look up at the hand, of course, and he just goes bang with the other hand. I'm thinking, nice one Gaz. Then he does a bit of Muhammad Ali dancing. I'm watching his feet move and then he goes bang, bang! And I go 'Good one, Gaz!' So, he's landed a couple on me and I'm amazed that I'm still standing but thinking to myself, better not throw any back coz I don't want to get him any angrier than he already is. So I'm dodging and weaving until about a minute and a half into the second round, when out of pure reflex and as true as I am sitting here writing this book, I throw a little left jab that catches him flush on the chin and drops him. The great man's eyes roll, he goes all limp and then falls to the canvas like a shot rhinoceros.

There he is, lying right in front of me in a crumpled heap. I'm looking down at him and thinking to myself, 'Oh, shit!' coz I know what's going to happen and so does the growing crowd of blokes who have, by this stage, all dropped their weights and come over to watch. They form a tight circle

Why don't you ever see baby pigeons?

around us. It's so tight that I can't get out. Next thing you know, Gazza quickly jumps up, gives a shake of the head and then proceeds to punch the living suitcases out of me. He throws every left hand–right hand combination, every uppercut and every blow to the body known to man. He even chucks in a few kickboxing moves for good measure. Just as other players are yelling out stuff like, 'You're going well Billy,' you'd hear, bang! and I'd cop another one to the head. 'Hang in there, Billy!' Bang! Another blow to the noggin. Pretty soon all the voices blur into one slow, warbled, dull sound. Although, you can still hear Paul Couch giggling (which isn't a surprise coz that's all he ever does). The crowd noise is finally broken by the sound of the new-fandangled timer going off. But I don't think Gazza hears it coz he begins to lift his attack up a notch. My head's popping back and forth like a cash register drawer. Eventually, Phillip Walsh forces his way through the circle of my team-mates and into the ring. He manages to pull Gazza off me and settle him down, while palming me out the back to the safety of the change rooms.

I'm sitting there, slumped on a bench in the change rooms, too numb to move and feeling like I've been punched into the next millennium. After much struggling I eventually get my gloves off. My head guard, on the other hand, isn't going to be as easy to remove. It's copped such a belting that the head guard is now imbedded in my head. It and my head have become one. Two hours pass before the swelling in my head has gone down enough for it to be removed.

For a good week afterwards, I still had the imprint of the head guard stitching on my face. Needless to say, Gazza got the points.

Billy on the big issues

THE BIG BANG THEORY

According to scientists, the universe started after a 'big bang'. So, first there was nothing, then there was a big bang and then there was everything. We're paying scientists all this money and that's the best they can come up with? What sort of lazy, half-arsed theory is that? Just because each of us came about from a big bang doesn't mean the whole universe did. Surely they could've done better than that. What, were they under pressure to get an answer out quickly? Did they want to rush home to turn on their Bunsen burners? Were they running late for footy training? Come on, guys! Put a bit of thought into it. Besides, it's not even an original idea. I was using it back when I was a kid. Mum would come into my bedroom, take one look at the mess and go, 'What happened here?' I'd say, 'It was a big bang, Mum. First there was no mess, then a big bang, then a whole heap of mess.'

How could you have a big bang that was big enough to start the whole universe, anyway? You'd need a shitload of fireworks for starters. At least as much as they use on the Sydney Harbour Bridge on New Year's Eve and then some. Maybe God got hold of a box of illegal fireworks, was mucking around and stuck a penny banger down the back of Adam's pants and bang! Instant universe.

EVOLUTION

Are we the descendants of apes? Well, they've dug up bones and found that humans changed over millions of years. They started off with a smaller brain and walking on all fours and then, over time, stood upright and had a much bigger brain (Adelaide supporters are still somewhere in the middle). So, based on what they've pulled out of the ground, it looks like we did come from apes or ape-like creatures (Cameron Ling from orang-utans). This does not discredit those people who believe that God made the world. Although, I reckon it would have taken him a lot longer than seven days (I hear he came in way over budget as well). When he was done, God must have sat back over a beer and had a good look at the earth and been pretty happy with himself. Not a bad effort for one bloke with a bad back. And this was way before nail guns or Supa Glue were invented.

ALIENS

Go outside at night and look up into the sky. See all the stars. There are millions of them. Our sun is just one of those stars. If the sun supports life on this planet and there are heaps more like it, I reckon there's a good chance that there's life somewhere out there. Will we ever have contact with aliens? I thought I did the night Geelong won the flag and I was lying in the gutter in a drunken stupor. Turns out I was just looking up at Paul Chapman's bald head in front of some car headlights (in my defence he was muttering the words 'phone home … phone home').

We are sending out radio signals to see if we get a response from outer space. So far, nothing. Maybe the aliens haven't got FM yet. Maybe our message went straight to their voice mail. We need to send them something that will get them excited to the point where they have to respond. I'm thinking the Richmond theme song. Everyone loves the Tigerland song. They won't be able to resist. When it gets to the bit that goes 'For we're from Tiger …' guaranteed the aliens will be straight back with 'yellow and black!'

THE MEANING OF LIFE

Why are we here? I'm not sure. To witness a Geelong premiership, maybe? We've finally done that, so does that mean we can pack everything up and go now? I suppose life means different things to different people. People who are religious have it all worked out. Their religion gives them a reason to be here. Life, I think, is to be enjoyed, experienced and, most importantly, respected. Sure, every now and again I do stop and think about why I'm here but life's too short. If you spend too much time thinking about stuff, then you'll miss out on enjoying yourself.

Be true to yourself and be good to others. I reckon if we all do that, then we've pretty much got it covered. Maybe I should start my own religion. I'd better start working on some songs. All religions need good songs.

LIFE AFTER DEATH

There are so many stories of people who claim that they died and then saw a bright light, before being revived and brought back to life. This has happened to a lot of people on the operating table. Mmmm … when you're being operated on there's usually a bright light right above you. What else did they see? A couple of doctors and a nurse, maybe?

Throughout history people have been preparing themselves and others for life after death. The ancient Egyptians built huge pyramids as tombs for their Pharaohs and would put all of their belongings in there, so that they could use them in the afterlife. We don't think like that anymore. There wouldn't be enough room in a coffin for my esky let alone the widescreen TV or my car.

There are people who believe in reincarnation. When we die we come back as something else on this earth, depending on how we lived our life. Which for me would mean that I'll be coming back as a stubbie holder.

I suppose there can only be life after death if our soul can be separated from the rest of our body. Is that possible? We're pretty weird creatures who are very different from other living things. Who knows? I'm happy to kick on somewhere else. I just hope the weather's nice there. Not too hot though, coz that would mean that I was in the other place.

Billy's premiership diary

29 September 2007. At the start of the year, that was just a date on my calendar. It was a Saturday that came between the 28th and the 30th. Who would have thought that when that day came around, it was to be the most momentous day of my life? (Apologies to the Darl. The wedding was great but it didn't make me shed a tear.) That's right, I cried on the 29th, I won't deny it. Well, I can't deny it. Millions of people around Australia and the world saw me bawling my eyes out on national television. The occasion just brought out all of the emotion in me. They were tears of joy, mixed with tears of relief. What a day, not only for me but for the players, all of the supporters and the town itself. It was a great day for Geelong.

For me, it wasn't just about that one day. It started back in 1986 when I made my debut for Geelong and then went on to play in four losing grand finals. Experiences like that are etched in your memory forever. They travel with you wherever you go. You can't shake them. My time at the football club was sensational but those losing grand finals burned in my guts. They really hurt. Well, they did until the mighty Cats pulled it off in 2007. That eased the pain and made me feel like my contribution was part of the journey to the premiership. I was a proud man that day, a very proud man.

LYREBIRD
AFL
SHERRIN

My build-up to Grand Final day started, like for most footy fans, with the Brownlow Medal on the Monday night. The Brownlow is always a top night, in between the vote counting bits. And don't the girls love it. It's more and more becoming their night. Pretty soon us blokes won't even need to turn up. It'd be a shame because it's always a good opportunity for the football community to get together and have a chat with each other. You really don't get much of a chance throughout the year. Gary Ablett Junior was the favourite but he was tipped out by none other than Geelong's other star midfielder, Jimmy Bartel. I felt sorry for Gary Jnr, he'd had a great year and all the focus was on him. Nevertheless, Jimmy Bartel was a worthy winner and a great bloke at that. It turned into another Geelong dominated awards night. Joel Selwood had already won the NAB Rising Star award and we had nine representatives in the All Australian Team. That's quite an achievement. It's not easy getting into the All Australian Team. I should know. I made it in 1991. One of the most expensive bribes I've ever paid out.

After kicking up my heels at the Brownlow, which went into Tuesday, I decided to have a think about planning my week. In a stroke of genius, I decided that I needed a central base for what was going to be a massive week. I booked into Crown Casino on the Wednesday and that became my home away from home for the next 4 or 5 days. Often you can stay at a hotel for a night and control yourself from getting stuck into the mini-bar, but 4 or 5 days was going to be pretty tough. This was going to really test me.

That night we went to the Channel Ten Seriously party. For some reason, all of the Channel Nine footy boys crack an invite. It's always a huge night and this one was no exception.

The who's who of media and footy were there and there was plenty of talk about the Cats. I was starting to get pretty excited and nervous at the same time. I probably threw back one too many that evening, can't really remember what time I stumbled into my room but I do have a vague memory of nearly tripping over a midget at the party ... or was that another party I popped in to on the way home? Not sure. (Stop press: I just worked out this would have been Rima from *Big Brother*!)

Thursday morning I was up and raring to go for the 1116 SEN breakfast show and then off to Rod Laver Arena to rehearse for that night's Grand Final edition of *The Footy Show*. I have never been a good singer (or mimer for that matter) and I dance like an elephant who's been shot with a tranquiliser dart but they still make me do these stupid routines every year. The atmosphere of a packed Tennis Centre is unbelievable. I wasn't feeling that confident with my song that year. I was Meat Loaf and I was doing 'Bat Out of Hell'. Not sure who saw the resemblance between me and Meat Loaf but no-one at the *The Footy Show* was prepared to own up to the idea. But being the true professional I am, once those lights came on and the music started, away I went. I was busting moves like there was no tomorrow. Don't get me wrong, I have no doubt it was crap but I haven't watched it back and don't plan to.

After the show we headed over to the Lexus Centre for the after party. Nice place Ed's got there. He's managed to build a monument to his own footy team. It's pretty impressive inside. It's got everything that opens and shuts. All the latest equipment, machines and facilities to give Collingwood that extra edge over the other clubs. I unplugged a few machines while I was there, hoping to set them back a couple of days in their preparations for the following year. Needless to say, we pretty much got on it again that night, for the third time that week ... and the Grand Final was still two days away!

I was up Friday morning at 5 am feeling very seedy and struggling to stay awake. On the radio, I was trying to pump up my own tyres regarding my performance on the previous night's *Footy Show* but the listeners soon let my tyres down by reminding me of just how terrible I was. After leaving 1116 SEN, with my ego completely pummelled and battered beyond recognition, I headed to a Western Bulldogs Grand Final lunch at the Carlton Crest. David Smorgon spoke well and left a good impression on me. There was also a really good illusionist there but I can't remember his name. I wanted to really test him out and see if he could make Jason Akermanis's hair and beard look the same colour.

Believe it or not, that night I attended a Port Adelaide supporters' Grand Final eve function. My good mate Dwayne Russell somehow talked me into it. He's an old Port boy. I think he was only taking me to offer me up to the Port supporters as a human sacrifice to bring good luck before the game. After the dinner I caught up with my two brothers, Blair and Anson, for a few pre-game beers (like I needed any more). The anticipation was really starting to build inside me. I couldn't wait for the next day.

Saturday morning I woke up next to Blair in the only double bed in the room. It's a nice room at Crown, so I figured I may as well use every inch of it. Blair wasn't really up for a cuddle, so I got out and I was off to the Channel Nine Grand Final breakfast. I tucked into it there and then I popped over to the G at 11 am to take part in the Foster's Obstacle Race.

I came last but considering the week I'd had, I was lucky to even finish. From there I headed to the September Club for a couple of speaking engagements. I got through those and took a seat for a bit of a breather. I checked my watch. It was just after 1 pm. I thought to myself, This is it! The moment had finally arrived. It was time to take up my pozzy at the ground and settle in.

I wanted to watch the game by myself. My own experiences, emotions and reasons for being there were very personal. I was going to need to be on my own for this. I decided the best place for me would be at the back of the 1116 SEN commentary box. It meant that I was there and could soak up the atmosphere but I still had my own space.

We all know what happened from there. Along with the other 90 000 spectators, I witnessed one of the greatest Geelong performances of all time. I just sat there and marvelled at every bit of play, every mark, every kick, every handball and every goal. By half-time the game was over and it was just a matter of sitting back and enjoying the next hour of football. It was a privilege to watch those boys run around that afternoon. They did the mighty Cats proud. The day we had been dreaming of for so long was here and in a big, big way.

When the siren went I was lucky enough to go out onto the ground and soak up the atmosphere of Geelong's first premiership in 44 years. It was an unbelievable feeling. It was awesome. Something I'll never forget. I became quite emotional and shed a few tears. Next thing you know there was a TV camera in my face. My personal experience was now in everyone's lounge room. At the time I didn't think too much about the crying. It just happened. Not sure why. It had been a long week, a huge build-up and I was pretty tired. It may also have had something to do with the fact that I love the club and gave my heart and soul to the place when I played there. That plus the heartache of those four losing grand finals. It all just came together after the victory and then came out of me. That day meant a lot to me.

I had turned my phone off before the game. I didn't want any interruptions. When I switched it back on after the game there were 73 text messages and eighteen phone messages. They all said 'congratulations' and 'well done' … and 'gee, you're a big sook'.

There were great scenes in the change rooms when the boys finally made it in with that premiership cup. There were a lot of smiling faces in there. Faces that were around when I was playing. It was a nice moment. I hung around and had a few beers with the boys. I certainly needed a couple myself. Then it was on to Federation Square. It was absolutely packed. I don't know how many times the Geelong theme song was sung but it sounded better each time. It was starting to dawn on me just what this premiership meant to so many people. No time for stopping and thinking, though. It was off to Crown for dinner.

I did a lot of drinking that night. And can you really blame me? I had a fair bit to celebrate. There was no room for half-measures. It was go all-out or go home. I did get a couple of hours' sleep, then it was up early for the *Sunday Footy Show*. I was doing a live cross from the Lord of Isles hotel in Geelong. That was the easy part. The hard part was trying to find two Geelong players to do the live cross with. After going to a few different houses I managed to track down the Norm Smith

The Cats paraded the cup through the streets of Geelong with President Frank Costa leading the way.

Medallist, Steven Johnson, and Andrew Mackie. All things considered, the cross, that nearly didn't happen, went well.

I went from there to Skilled Stadium to help out with the Geelong Family Day. The atmosphere was incredible. Those die-hard supporters, who are the backbone of this great club, were in their element. They were having the time of their lives. Everyone was singing the theme song and still high-fiving and hugging anyone they could. It was a beautiful thing to see. I'll never forget standing on the stage looking out at 36 000 ecstatic Geelong fans packed onto the ground and into the stands. The players were in fine form too by this stage. Fuelled by alcohol, no sleep, sheer excitement and adrenalin, the boys were jumping up and down and egging the crowd on. Best on stage for me was Max Rooke who was the only player to still have his official Geelong Football Club suit on from the previous day.

From the family day about twenty of us past players went back to the Lord of the Isles hotel to reminisce about the good old days. The next five hours were nearly the best of the whole week. Many of the fans from the family day also ended up at the pub and it was starting to slowly fill right up. Every 15 minutes one of the past players had to get up on the fireplace and sing the theme song. The whole pub got involved and the passion and love for one another were fantastic. After a couple of hours I actually thought that I'd played in the Grand Final.

At about 11 pm I had the wobbly boots on and had to ring the Darl, who came and picked me up. Gee, I was a happy boy. What a great week. It'll be pretty hard to top, I reckon.

*** Footnote:** Trust Geelong supporters to think of a way to keep the celebrations going. Many of them are still having regular dinner gatherings at their homes called 'Victory Parties'. They invite other Geelong supporters around and they all have to wear their Geelong gear. When everyone sits down at the dinner table, the Grand Final DVD goes on. After toasting each goal, each person at the table has to stand up and tell the group what the premiership meant to them. The night, of course, wouldn't be complete without a rousing rendition of the Geelong theme song. A mate of mine went to one that was so well organised they had the Geelong mascot, 'Half Cat', turn up. Everyone had their photo taken with Half Cat and the night ended up going into the wee hours of the morning. Now that's how to celebrate a premiership!

The silo story: the final truth

The story of me kicking a footy over a wheat silo has been doing the rounds for years. It's one of the first questions people ask me when they meet me (that and 'Where's the wheel?'). Did it really happen or is the silo story just the stuff of myth and legend? Well, right here and now, I'm finally going to come clean on it. This is it. The definitive story on the silo. What you are about to read is the truth, the whole truth and nothing but the truth, so help me Gazza.

I was a bright-eyed young kid, having just played my first year down at Geelong. Back in the days when I was skinny and had hair. It was the off-season and me and a couple of mates from Assumption College were going to another mate's (Flaggy's) wedding up at West Wyalong. But first we had to drop in to Jerilderie to 'borrow' Mum's car coz all I had was a shitty little Gemini, which, like a long shot in the Melbourne Cup, would struggle to make the journey. So, into her car we got (with a few travellers, of course) and off we went.

We're making pretty good time and enjoying each other's company, as you do in the bush, when, all of a sudden, out of nowhere, this magnificent looking two storey pub pops up. It looks like it was built in the early 1900s. It's made of red brick with yellow brick trim and has ornate metal work around the balcony. I can hear it calling me. 'Billy … Billy … get in here, big fella!'

You wouldn't believe it, the car hits a bump, we lose control and bang, we look up and we're right out the front of the pub. So, we think to ourselves, we may as well have a couple of beers while we're here. It's your classic country pub. It has a warm, homely feel, not much natural light and some well worn furniture. There are some pinball machines down one end and a general store for all of your bread and milk needs down the other. The 60-year-old, grey haired publican is leaning over the bar with a big friendly smile on his face. He looks like he was born and raised behind that bar. 'Where are we, mate?' I ask him. 'Mirrool,' he replies. 'Population: 28.' He's poured three pots before we've got the words out of our mouths. We prop ourselves up on some stools at the bar and start to settle in.

Three shouts into our session, I notice a flat-looking footy resting on a shelf behind the bar. So I say to the publican, 'Hey, Cocko, what's the story with that footy behind the bar, mate?' His eyes light up like he's about to tell a story he really enjoys sharing. 'See that silo across the road?' We all turn together like synchronised swimmers and through the window we can see the base of this huge silo. We can't see the top. It goes out of sight, past the edge of the window. The publican continues, 'A few years ago, an Aboriginal bloke, on his way through from Darwin, kicked this footy over that silo. A lot of blokes have tried since, and I mean a lot of blokes, but nobody's been able to do it.' We wander out and take a closer look at the

If a synchronised swimmer drowns, do the rest drown too?

silo. We gaze up in amazement. It's got to be 40 metres high, which makes that young man from Darwin's feat even more impressive. Back to the bar we head.

A couple of beers later and you can start to feel the confidence building. We're sitting taller in our stools and our chests are sticking out. Something inside is telling me that we're going to have a crack at this! The publican can see it in our eyes too. 'What are you boys waiting for? Here ya go!' With that, he hands us the footy. It's as flat as a tack. He gestures to a couple of kids who are playing the pinnies. They grab the ball, run home, pump it up and run back.

There we all are, lined up on the railway station platform in front of the silo. Our suits for the wedding are in the car, so we're still in shorts and bare feet. I'm kicking first and am spinning the ball in my hands as I gaze up at the silo, which now looks twice as high as it did before. The publican delivers his final words of encouragement: 'There's free piss if you can kick the ball over.' I'm ready, I think to myself. Let's do this! I take a couple of steps before launching into a drop punt, as hard as I can (a torpedo wouldn't get the height). There's a weird silence as everyone watches the ball head towards the top of the silo. Before you know it, it sails right over and out of sight. I can't believe it! The boys who had been playing the pinnies earlier were waiting on the other side and they come running back around with the footy, saying 'He's done it, he's done it!' I'm pretty happy with myself. I've done it with one kick and one kick only.

Without waiting another minute, I go straight back to the pub, where, all of a sudden, the publican's my best mate. He's giving me free grog and the next thing you know, I'm signing beer coasters and toilet doors. It's a good hour later before my mates arrive back at the pub. They've given up after heaps of attempts, frustration and sunburn taking a toll on them. Nothing a few more beers won't fix.

Fortunately, one of us remembers that we actually have a wedding to go to. None of us are in any condition to get behind the wheel, so with my newly found celebrity status, we manage to convince one of the locals to drive us. Off to West Wyalong we head. Finding the church proves difficult and we're already running late. As we turn a corner, the church just pops up out of nowhere (just like the pub had earlier). We chuck our penguin suits on and run in. The ceremony has already started but we manage to sneak in and sit up the back without causing too much disruption.

The vibe in the church is certainly different to where we've just come from. It's a very proper ceremony. The bride looks stunning in a long flowing white gown. The boys are all giving her the thumbs up. Problem is, the groom looks nothing like Flaggy. We all look at each other. We're at the wrong wedding.

I've now officially written one more book than I've read.

Hooroo

Picture credits

All photographs in the colour picture section and on the following pages are by James Penlidis: pages 44, 68, 75, 131, 153, 178, 184

Map on page 22 and plumbing diagram on page 88 are by Guy Holt.

Page (i):Neville Bruns looks on as Bill Brownless kicks, 15 March 1986

Page 49: 1986, Bill Brownless in the squad for the Big V (but didn't make the final cut); courtesy *Geelong Advertiser*.

Page 50: Billy Brownless flies over top of Ashley MacIntosh as he goes for mark during Geelong v West Coast Eagles, 1 October 1994; photographer John Feder, courtesy of Newspix.

Page 52: Geelong coach Malcolm Blight from 1989, courtesy of Newspix.

Page 66: Geelong's Billy Brownless kicks the winning goal after the siren, 9 September 1994; photographer George Salpigtidis, courtesy of Newspix.

Page 85: Courtesy of *Geelong Advertiser*.

Page 93: Ted Whitten with his son during a lap of honour before the State of Origin match at the MCG, 17 June 1995; courtesy of Newspix.

Page 108: Stills of Billy's wheel courtesy of Channel Nine's Footy Show.

Page 118: Date unknown; courtesy of Newspix

Page 122: Coach Malcolm Blight talks to Gary Ablett, 8 July 1990; photographer Brett Faulkner, courtesy of Newspix.

Page 126: Bill Brownless takes a well-earned rest after starring against Fitzroy, 25 April 1987; photographer Colin Bull; courtesy of Newspix.

Page 190: Geelong Football Club Grand Final parade through Geelong, club president Frank Costa with the cup, 3 October 2007; courtesy of Newspix.

Thanks

Great big thanks to Nicky (the love of my life). Marrying the Darl and having the kids have been my greatest achievements by far. Fortunately we have a few things in common. She loves a beer and a bet and makes a mean pav. She loves to cook and I love to eat – we're a match made in heaven. She keeps things running smoothly at home while I pretty much come and go. Thankfully she is pretty understanding and she's done a fantastic job of raising the kids: Lucy, Ruby, Oscar and Max. So far the journey has been great and I wouldn't change a thing (except maybe winning one of those Grand Finals).

Thanks to Tim Watson and Andrew Maher, and all the listeners of our breakfast show, Morning Glory, on Melbourne's 1116 SEN – great ideas, guys.

Thanks to Paul Calleja – couldn't have done it without you, mate. And to my publisher Andrea McNamara (who reminds me of a Year 9 teacher who used to nag me for my homework). And to the mysterious Pauline Haas who made it all into a book (another example of how women do all the work but men get all the credit).

Thanks to everyone at Channel Nine and Geelong Football Club, past and present. And to Ned, Boxy and Nudge at ESP for keeping me in line.

And thanks to all those blokes I've had a beer with or stood around a BBQ with all my life. You all know who you are.

And, of course, I'd like to thank my parents, especially Mum and Dad.